INTERNATIONAL DIMENSIONS OF MANAGEMENT

The Kent
International Business Series

DAVID A. RICKS

Series Consulting Editor

KENT PUBLISHING COMPANY
A Division of Wadsworth, Inc.
Boston, Massachusetts

INTERNATIONAL DIMENSIONS OF MANAGEMENT

Arvind V. Phatak
Temple University

This book is dedicated to
Rhoda, Vikram, Rajesh, and Viveca

Editor: John B. McHugh
Production Editor: Tina Samaha
Cover and Text Designer: Armen Kojoyian
Production Coordinator: Linda Siegrist

Kent Publishing Company
A Division of Wadsworth, Inc.

Printed in the United States of America
3   4   5   6   7   8   9—86   85

Library of Congress Cataloging in Publication Data

Phatak, Arvind V.
    International dimensions of management.

    (The Kent international business series)
    Includes bibliographies and index.
    1. International business enterprises—Management.
2. Industrial management.   I. Title.   II. Series.
HD62.4.P52   1983   658'.049   82-17131
ISBN 0-534-01317-1

Series Foreword

Prior to World War II, the number of firms involved in foreign direct investment was relatively small. Although several U.S. companies were obtaining raw materials from other countries, most firms were only interested in the U.S. market. This changed, however, during the 1950s—especially after the creation of the European Economic Community. Since that time, there has been a rapid expansion in international business activity.

The majority of the world's large corporations now perform an increasing proportion of their business activities outside of their home country. For many of these companies, international business returns over one-half of their profits, and it is becoming more and more common for a typical corporation to earn at least one-fourth of its profits through international business involvement. In fact, it is now rather rare for any large firm not to be a participant in the world of international business.

International business is of great importance in most countries and that importance continues to grow. To meet the demand for increased knowledge in this area, business schools are attempting to add international dimensions to their curricula. Faculty members are becoming more interested in teaching a greater variety of international business courses and are striving to add international dimensions to other courses. Students, aware of the increasing probability that they will be employed by firms engaged in international business activities, are seeking knowledge of the problem-solving techniques unique to international business. As the American Assembly of Collegiate Schools of Business has observed, however, there is a shortage of information available. Most business textbooks do not adequately consider the international dimensions of business and much of the supplemental material is disjointed, overly narrow or otherwise inadequate in the classroom.

This series has been developed to overcome such problems. The books are written by some of the most respected authors in the various areas of international business. Each author is extremely well known in the Academy of International Business and in his other professional academies. Each possesses an outstanding knowledge of his subject matter and a talent for explaining it.

These books, in which the authors have identified the most important international aspects of their fields, have been written in a format which facilitates their use as supplemental material in business school courses. For the most part, the material is presented by topic in approximately the same order and manner as it is covered in basic business textbooks. Therefore, as each topic is covered in the course, material is easily supplemented with the corresponding chapter in the series book.

The Kent Series in International Business offers a unique and much needed opportunity to bring international dimensions of business into the classroom. The series has been developed by leaders in the field after years of discussion and careful consideration, and the timely encouragement and support provided by Keith Nave, Kent Senior Editor on this project. I am proud to be associated with this series and highly recommend it to you.

David A. Ricks

Consulting Editor to the
Kent Series in International Business
Professor of International Business,
University of South Carolina

Preface

The dramatic growth of international business which began soon after the Second World War shows no signs of abating. The multinational corporation has been, and continues to be, the most important force promoting this growth. U.S. multinational companies alone account for over $200 billion of foreign direct investments, and it is estimated that these investments control total assets of over $500 billion. The enormity of the impact of multinational corporations on the global economy becomes visible when one considers an estimate made by the International Chamber of Commerce that U.S. multinationals, by themselves, churn out one-third of the gross world product.

We now live in a world in which the economies of nations are closely intertwined because of the international transactions of both large and small multinational corporations. Present-day graduates of business schools may well establish their careers in multinational corporations, and those who do not will surely have to deal with multinational corporations in one way or another. Therefore it is imperative that business graduates have a good understanding of how multinational corporations operate and of the nature of the managerial tasks in such enterprises.

The basic premise of this book is that management of a company having international operations differs in many ways from that of a company doing business within the boundries of just one country. All the material in this book is concerned with the managerial issues confronting the top management executives as they attempt to plan, organize, staff, and control the global operations of the multinational company. The focus throughout this book is upon *management* functions, as opposed to enterprise functions (finance, marketing, accounting, and production). Emphasis is on the management functions in an international company which are significantly different from those in a purely domestic company.

The purpose of this book is to provide the reader with an appreciation of the international dimensions of the management process. It can not contain an exhaustive coverage of the international management field. Rather, it is designed as a supplementary text in introductory graduate or undergraduate general management courses with the objective of internationalizing the course content.

Several people have helped me during the various phases of writing this book. I wish to extend my gratitude to my graduate assistant Kathleen Filano, who so very diligently helped me in obtaining the required materials and in proofreading the manuscript. I also thank the staff in the Research Center of the School of Business of Temple University, particularly Janet Danelutti, for organizing the manuscript typing, and Pamela Bennett, Shelah Burgess, and Ernestine Hopson for typing it so expeditiously.

Contents

Chapter 1

An Introduction to International Management

The need for international management arises when a company becomes involved in foreign direct investment. Direct investment is a long-term equity investment in a foreign firm; it gives the parent company (the investor) managerial control over the foreign firm. Direct investments abroad by U.S. companies at the end of 1978 were in excess of $168 billion, and those by foreign companies in the United States amounted to more than $40 billion.[1] The magnitude of these investment outlays becomes apparent when one compares them with the gross national product figures of countries. For example, in 1978 the gross national product—which is the value of all final goods and services produced by a nation's economy—of every country of the world, excluding the ten wealthiest, was less than $120 billion; and that of every country, excluding the twenty-five wealthiest, was less than $40 billion.[2]

International management activities in a firm begin when the firm's managers either initiate the establishment of a foreign affiliate from scratch or buy an existing firm; and they continue as long as there are one or more functioning foreign affiliates owned by the parent company.

Throughout this book, when we consider the elements of international management our subject will always be the so-called international or multinational firm or company. Many scholars of international business make a distinction between an international and a multinational company. However, we shall be using the terms interchangeably. Also used synonymously are the terms *affiliate* and *subsidiary;* in addition, we make no distinction among these terms: *company, corporation, enterprise,* and *firm.*

WHAT IS INTERNATIONAL BUSINESS?

There are many different definitions of international business. First, let us see what some of them are, and then we shall arrive at our own definition. John Fayerweather says that international business has "only one central distinguishing characteristic—it is business involving two or more nations."[3] John Daniels, Earnest W. Ogram, Jr., and Lee H. Radebaugh define it as "either private or governmental business relationships conducted across national boundaries."[4] Richard Farmer and Barry Richman define it as "business operations of any sort by one firm, which take place within or between two or more independent countries."[5] There are many such definitions of international business. We shall define international business as those business activities of private or public enterprises that involve the movement across national boundaries of resources, goods, services, and skills. The resources that are involved in the transfer are raw materials, capital, people, and technology; goods transferred include semifinished and finished assemblies and products; services transferred include such things as accounting, legal counsel, and banking activities; and skills sent from one country to another include managerial and technical skills.

INTERNATIONAL MANAGEMENT DEFINED

In very general terms, international management is the *management* of a firm's activities on an international scale. Before we define international management, let us define the term *management.*

Management is the process aimed at accomplishing organizational objectives by: (1) effectively coordinating the procurement, allocation, and utilization of human and physical resources of the organization; and (2) maintaining the organization in a state of dynamic equilibrium with the environment. There are two basic premises in this definition of management. First, management is needed to coordinate the human and physical resources—the raw materials, capital, technology, knowledge—and to integrate them into a unified whole. Without such coordination the resources would remain unrelated and disorganized, therefore inefficiently used. The second premise in the definition is that an organization lives in a dynamic environment that constantly affects its operations. Thus, one managerial task is to forecast the environmental forces that are likely to have a significant impact on the firm in the immediate and distant future, and to determine the probable impact of these forces. Managers must design appropriate strategies to ensure the survival and growth of the organization as it interacts with its dynamic environment.

On the basis of the preceding definition of management, we can now define *international management* as the process of accomplishing the global objectives of an organization by: (1) effectively coordinating the procurement, allocation, and utilization of the human and physical resources of the organization; and (2) maintaining the organization in a state of dynamic equilibrium within the global environment.

INTERNATIONAL MANAGEMENT AND MULTINATIONAL COMPANIES

Any firm that has one or more foreign affiliates is involved in international management; it does not have to be a billion dollar corporation. Even small and medium-sized firms can and do have international operations in several countries. Many multinationals do not qualify for the exclusive list of the *Fortune 500* or the *Forbes 100* list of the largest U.S. and foreign multinationals. Even though they do not come close to Ford and General Motors in terms of total sales, gross profits, total assets, and other similar measures of company size, they are still multinational companies. Many firms in Europe and Japan have also developed a multinational structure; and in the last ten years or so, we have seen many government-owned enterprises that have become multinational.

The 1960s laid the foundations for the massive growth abroad of U.S. multinational enterprises. The growth of that decade far exceeded any achieved earlier by the United States or the other industrialized countries of the world. Direct investments abroad by American business enterprises surged from $31.8 billion in 1960 to $78 billion in 1970, and they exceeded $168 billion in 1978. However, those dollar values of foreign direct investments are the values carried on the books of U.S. parent companies; but book value is the value of the investment at the time it was made, not adjusted to the changes in price due to inflation. Because inflation has been a global phenomenon since World War II, the book values of U.S. direct investments made ten or twenty years ago grossly understate their current replacement values. The current market price of U.S. direct investments abroad is much higher.

The massive outflow of U.S. direct investments in the 1960s represented the response by U.S. companies to business opportunities in foreign markets. The nature of the response had been dramatically different in the decades before the sixties. U.S. exports to foreign markets was replaced by direct production of the goods in company-owned plants located in the foreign market itself. This strategy of establishing production affiliates in foreign countries to serve one or more foreign markets was responsible for the growth and development of multinational enterprises—first in the United States and later in Western Europe and Japan. Today the value of U.S. exports is dwarfed by the value of goods produced in U.S.-owned foreign affiliates. The sales figures of the foreign affiliates owned by U.S. companies are about four times the value of U.S. exports, and it is estimated that almost one-half of the industrial output of the noncommunist world today is produced by firms that have developed a multinational structure.[6] U.S. multinationals are now playing the dominant role in the proliferation of U.S. business abroad and in the production and marketing of American products in foreign countries.

Although multinational enterprises are dissimilar in many respects—such as size of sales and profits, markets served, and location of affiliates abroad—they all do have some common features. To begin, a multinational company is an enterprise that has a network of wholly or partially (jointly with one or more foreign partners) owned producing and marketing affiliates located in a number of countries. The foreign affiliates are linked with the parent company and with each other by ties of common ownership and by a common global strategy to which each affiliate is responsive and committed. The parent company controls the foreign affiliates via resources which it allocates to each affiliate—such as capital, technology, trademarks, patents, and manpower—and through the right to approve each affiliate's long- and short-range plans and budgets.

As pointed out earlier, there are many small and medium-sized multinational companies. However, generally we are talking about a large corporation whose revenues and assets typically run into hundreds of millions of dollars. For example, each of the ten largest U.S. multinationals has revenues in excess of $23 billion dollars; the revenues of each of the one hundred largest U.S. multinationals have surpassed the $2 billion mark. Similarly, the revenues of each of the ten largest foreign multinationals have exceeded $23 billion. The total assets of each of the five largest U.S. multinational companies exceed $22 billion, and their combined assets exceed $162 billion.

Another characteristic of multinational companies is that they own a large number of foreign affiliates. The largest 200 multinationals in the world have affiliates in twenty or more countries.

Multinational companies tend to gravitate toward certain types of business activities. Most multinational companies are engaged in the manufacturing sector, with petroleum running a distant second. Other industries in which multinationals are involved include banking, mining, agriculture, and public utilities.

A large proportion of the total business activities of multinational companies are located in the developed countries of Western Europe, Canada, and the U.S. It is estimated that about two-thirds of the world's direct investments are in the developed countries.

As for their operations in the manufacturing sector, multinational companies are particularly strong in certain kinds of industries, often holding a dominant position in drugs, chemicals, electronics, food processing, petroleum refining, synthetic fibers, and electrical equipment.

THE ENVIRONMENT OF INTERNATIONAL MANAGEMENT

A manager in an international company performs her or his managerial functions in an environment that is far more complex than that of her or his counterpart in a domestic company. The international environment is the total world environment. However, it is also the sum total of the environments of every nation in which the company has its foreign affiliates. The environment within each nation consists of four basic elements: legal, cultural, economic, and political. Exhibit 1-1 shows the variables typically found in each element of the environment.

An international manager—at least, one who is responsible for managing the transfer of managerial, financial, material, technical, or hu-

EXHIBIT 1-1 *The International Environment*

Legal Environment	Cultural Environment
Legal tradition	Customs, norms,
Effectiveness of legal	values, beliefs
system	Language
Treaties with foreign	Attitudes
nations	Motivations
Patent trademark laws	Social institutions
Laws affecting business	Status symbols
firms	Religious beliefs

Economic Environment	Political System
Level of economic development	Form of government
Population	Political ideology
Gross national product	Stability of government
Per capita income	Strength of opposition
Literacy level	parties and groups
Social infrastructure	Social unrest
Natural resources	Political strife and
Climate	insurgency
Membership in regional economic	Governmental attitude
blocks (E.E.C.; L.A.F.T.A. . .)	towards foreign firms
Monetary and fiscal policies	Foreign policy
Nature of competition	
Currency convertability	
Inflation	
Taxation system	
Interest rates	
Wage and salary levels	

man resources and goods or services across national boundaries—should be continuously monitoring the environmental variables of the countries involved, especially those that may have a significant positive or negative impact. For example, a manager of international finance should study and evaluate the inflation rates, currency stability, and corporate tax levels of various countries before deciding how to minimize the foreign exchange losses when the company transfers money from an affiliate in one country to that in another.

Similarly, a decision to establish a manufacturing plant abroad will require a study of those environmental variables that would have a major impact on the operation and long-term survival of the plant in the foreign country—such as political stability, governmental attitude towards foreign firms, wage and salary levels, social infrastructure (roads, electricity, water, transportation) and per capita income. In addition, the decision to transfer a managerial technique from the parent company or foreign affiliate to another affiliate located in a different country must be preceded by an evaluation of the *relevant* environmental factors. For instance, a transfer of a leadership technique from one country to another must take into account the values, beliefs, attitudes, and motives of the people in the recipient country. For example, a participative leadership style may be effective in a culture whose values and beliefs are democratically oriented, but it may be wholly unworkable in a culture that respects authority and paternal influence.

Not only must the international manager monitor the environment of countries where the company currently has operations, but he or she must also make a continuous surveillance of other nations' environments. Both opportunities and threats can arise anywhere in the world, so it is important for management to stay on top of developments occurring in many different parts of the world.

One can say that the international environment of a firm is the world at large. However, on a smaller, "firm-specific" level, a multinational company's environment is that of the countries to which it transfers its resources, goods, or services.

DIFFERENT TYPES OF INTERNATIONAL BUSINESS

An international company can achieve its international business aims via different forms of activities—ranging from the import and export of resources, goods, and services to the production and marketing of products in foreign markets. Let us briefly examine these international business activities.

Direct Import and Export

A firm is involved in direct import and export when it directly imports goods from abroad and exports its goods to foreign buyers without the help of a middleperson or agency in the home country.

Portfolio Investment

Portfolio investment as an international business activity represents the transfer of funds across national boundaries by an international company for the purpose of buying the stocks, bonds, or notes issued by a foreign company, or the treasury notes or bills sold by a foreign government agency.

Contract Manufacturing

When a company engages in contract manufacturing, it enters into a contractual agreement with a foreign producer under which the foreign producer produces the company's product for sale in the foreign market. The company retains the responsibility for the promotion and distribution of its product.

Licensing

A foreign licensing agreement occurs when the international company, the licensor, agrees to make available to another company abroad, the licensee, use of its patents and trademarks, along with manufacturing process and know-how, trade secrets, and managerial and technical services. In exchange, the foreign company agrees to pay the licensor a royalty or other form of payment according to a schedule agreed upon by the two parties. The licensing agreement could be between the parent company of the international enterprise and one or more of its foreign affiliates; or it could be between the international enterprise and an independent foreign private or government enterprise.

Turnkey Projects

When an international company is engaged in setting up a turnkey operation abroad, it is responsible for the design and construction of the entire operation; on completion of the project, the total management of the operation is handed over to local personnel, who have been trained by the international company. In return for the completion of the project, the international company receives a fee, which can be quite substantial. International companies get involved in several types of turnkey projects: the construction of dams, electric power stations, and roads; and the building of factory complexes, such as steel mills, refineries, chemical plants, and automobile plants.

Several American and foreign companies have completed turnkey projects abroad. Bechtel and Fluor—two American companies—have constructed plants and construction projects in many countries; Rust Engineering Company is an American company that has constructed several chemical plants abroad, many of them in Eastern Europe. Fiat, the famous Italian company, has constructed an entire automobile plant in the Soviet Union.

Foreign Manufacturing

An international company engages in foreign manufacturing when it establishes a foreign manufacturing subsidiary. The foreign subsidiary may be wholly owned by the international company, or it may be a joint venture between it and one or more foreign business enterprises. The foreign business partners in a joint venture may be private companies or the host government. Several U.S., European, and Japanese companies have joint ventures with government-owned firms in the developing countries. The output of the foreign subsidiary may be geared to meet the domestic demand, or it may be designated in part or in total for export to markets in still other countries.

Typically an international company engages in all the preceding types of international business activities simultaneously in different areas of the world. As a company gradually evolves into a multinational company, the parent company of the international enterprise decides which of the international business activities each of the foreign affiliates is to be responsible for. Next we shall see how this evolution of a multinational enterprise takes place.

THE EVOLUTION OF A MULTINATIONAL ENTERPRISE

As a uninational (domestic) company evolves into a full-fledged multinational enterprise, it goes through several distinct but overlapping evolutionary stages. Some companies go through these stages quite rapidly—in a few years—whereas others may take many years to evolve into true multinationals. And all companies do not systematically proceed from one evolutionary stage to another; some in fact skip one or several of the stages.

Stage 1   The Foreign Inquiry

Stage one begins when a company receives an inquiry about one of its products directly from a foreign businessperson or from an independent domestic exporter and importer. The company may ignore the inquiry, in which case there is no further evolutionary development. However, if the company responds positively and has its product sold in the foreign market at a profit, then the stage is set for more sales of its products abroad; and the company executives probably become favorably disposed toward the export of their products. Other inquiries from foreign buyers are received more enthusiastically, and the company sells its products abroad through a domestic export middleperson. The middleperson could be an export merchant, an export commission house, a resident buyer (a buyer who is domiciled in the exporting company's home market and represents all types of private or governmental foreign buyers), a broker, a combination export manager (an exporter who serves as the exclusive export department of several noncompeting manufacturers), or a manufacturer's agent. (Unlike the combination export manager, who makes sales in the name of each company she or he represents, the manufacturer's agent retains her or his identity by operating in her or his own name).

Stage 2   The Export Manager

The company's exports continue to expand and the executives decide that the time is ripe to take the export management in their own hands and not to rely anymore on unsolicited inquiries from abroad. A decision is made to assume a proactive rather than a reactive posture towards exports. Hence, an export manager with a small staff is appointed to actively search for foreign markets for the company's products.

Stage 3   The Export Department and Direct Sales

As export sales continue their upward surge, the company has difficulty operating with only an export manager and his or her little staff. A full-fledged export department or division is established at the same level as the domestic sales department. The company drops the domestic export middleperson and starts to sell directly to importers or buyers located in foreign markets.

Stage 4   Sales Branches and Subsidiaries

Further growth of export sales requires the establishment of sales branches abroad to handle sales and promotional work. The sales branch manager is directly responsible to the home office and the branch sells directly to middlepersons in the foreign markets. The sales branch gradually evolves into a sales subsidiary that is incorporated and domiciled in the foreign country. It enjoys greater autonomy than the sales branch.

Stage 5   Assembly Abroad

The company may begin assembly operation in one or more of the foreign markets. The company may adopt this strategy if it is more profitable to export the disassembled product abroad rather than the whole product. Often tariffs and transportation costs are lower on unassembled parts and components than on the assembled finished product.

Stage 6   Production Abroad

By now the company has a well-developed export program and operation that is supported by country market studies, promotion and distribution programs tailored to the needs of each country market, and market research for the identification of new foreign markets.

The company's executives may now begin to experience difficulties in increasing the total sales volume and profit in foreign markets in which they currently have a foothold, or may find it impossible to enter other potentially lucrative markets via exports. This often occurs when the local governments impose very high tariffs or quotas on the import of certain products, or bans their import totally if the products are being produced locally by a domestic company. In such cases, the company executives decide to penetrate the foreign markets by producing the product right in the foreign market itself.

There are generally three different methods available for commencing foreign production: (1) contract manufacturing, (2) licensing, and (3) direct investment in manufacturing facilities. There are advantages and disadvantages to each of these methods; therefore the appropriate strategy or method will depend on the special circumstances of the company concerned.

Contract Manufacturing

By and large, U.S. companies have avoided contract manufacturing and have started with licensing and gradually moved toward direct investment in production facilities.

Licensing

If the company adopts the licensing route to foreign manufacturing, more often than not it finds licensing to be a less than satisfactory approach for penetrating the foreign market. The dissatisfaction of the company with licensing may come from the company executives' belief that the foreign licensee is not doing enough to promote sales of the licensed product, or that the licensee is not maintaining product quality (thus damaging the reputation and trademark of the company). There are many other reasons that could cause dissatisfaction with the licensee's performance and with the total licensing arrangement.[7] Even when the licensee performs well, the company may feel that it can do better financially and operationally without the licensee. For the licensor company, then, establishing a manufacturing facility via direct investment becomes an increasingly attractive method for tapping foreign markets.

Investment in Manufacturing

The company establishes a manufacturing facility in a foreign market. It now becomes involved with managing the total business in a foreign country. It must therefore perform the many business functions abroad—such as purchasing, finance, human resource planning and management, manufacturing, marketing, and so on. The company is also obligated to make significant commitments of technical, management, and financial resources to the new foreign entity.

The company learns from its experiences with the first foreign manufacturing venture, and this paves the way for the establishment of other foreign manufacturing plants abroad. At the same time, the company continues to export its products and to license its technology to foreign businesses and increasingly to its own foreign affiliates.

As the company matures as an international exporter, licensor, and producer of products, it meets the global demand for its products by exports from several of its foreign production affiliates, as well as by exports from the parent company and by the products of the foreign licensing arrangements. As the complexity of managing the geographically far-flung operations in several countries increases, the parent company managers recognize the benefits of integrating and tightening up the company's global operations and of managing the entire company as one global organizational system. The motivation to use the so-called systems approach in managing the company as one unit, with each foreign and domestic affiliate functioning as a subunit of the whole company, arises when several questions emerge to confront the company:

1. Which of the several foreign affiliates should export to a third country market?

2. Different affiliates operate in countries with differing inflation rates and corporate tax structures, so how should the financial resources of each affiliate be managed with the objective of maximizing the total global earnings of the entire company?

3. Can promotional expenditures be lowered by standardizing advertising internationally?

Questions such as these make the parent company management perceive the company as one global enterprise system and not merely as an aggregation of several domestic and foreign affiliates. When the parent company's management begins to see the advantages of making strategic decisions—in various functional areas, such as purchasing, finance, production, marketing, personnel, and research and development—from the perspective of the company as one integrated system, the stage is set for the company's evolution as a multinational enterprise.

Stage 7   Integration of Foreign Affiliates

The parent company managers decide to integrate the various foreign affiliates into one multinational enterprise system. The foreign affiliates lose considerable autonomy as strategic decisions are now made by top management at the company headquarters. The company's management begins to view the entire world as its theater of operations; it plans, organizes, staffs, and controls its international operations from a global perspective. Strategic decisions are made after a careful analysis of their worldwide implications: In what country should we build our next production facility? Throughout the world, where are our markets, and from which production center should they be served? From which sources in the world should we borrow capital to finance our current and future operations? Where should our research and development laboratories be located? From which countries should we recruit people? When the management of the company starts thinking and operating in global terms then it has evolved into a true multinational enterprise.

Not all companies go through each of the seven stages described in the preceding sections. Some companies stop short of complete integration of their domestic and foreign operations, preferring instead to manage their domestic and foreign operations in a decentralized manner, without an overall global strategy. Others may choose to coordinate the operations of affiliates in a certain region of the world, such as Europe, and keep the affiliates in other regions unattached and semiautonomous. Still other companies may decide to think globally with respect to only a few, and not all, of the enterprise functions. For instance, managers may think in worldwide terms when financial and production issues are concerned but not for marketing, personnel, purchasing, and research and development. Thus there are different degrees of multinationality in operation on a multinational scale. Some firms may progress further along the multinational path and become true multinationals, whereas others may choose to end their journey along the path at various milestones along the way.

Many changes in management practices and organizational structure occur as a firm evolves into a multinational company. Some of these changes involve a radical reorientation in the attitudes and values of the managers with respect to both the role of the company in the world economy and the allegiance of the company to the home country; another significant arena for change is the managers' perceptions of people of different nationalities, cultures, and races.

WHY INTERNATIONAL COMPANIES ENGAGE IN FOREIGN PRODUCTION

An international company may have several motivations for establishing foreign production facilities. Some of them have been alluded to in the preceding paragraphs on the evolution of multinational enterprises. Let us examine some of the other motivations for foreign production.

To protect and maintain a market position abroad, many companies have been forced to establish production facilities in foreign markets that once were served through exports but later were threatened with the imposition of high tariffs or quotas. The so-called voluntary restrictions of 1980 concerning exports to the United States of Japanese automobiles have prompted some of the Japanese auto companies to build car manufacturing plants in the United States. Similarly, many U.S. companies have established plants in the European Economic Community (EEC)—commonly known as the European Common Market—to jump over the common tariff and nontariff barriers raised by the member countries against imports from non–EEC countries.

Another reason companies set up foreign plants is to eliminate or reduce high transportation costs, particularly if the ratio of the per-unit transportation expenditures to the per-unit selling price of the product is very high. For instance, if the product costs $10 to ship but it can be marketed for no more than $25 in the foreign market, all other things being near equal, the company may decide to produce it in the market in order to improve its profit margin.

Rapid expansion of a foreign market for the company's product, along with the desire to obtain a large market share in it before a major competitor can get in are other strong driving forces for companies to engage in foreign production. There are many distinct advantages that a firm can enjoy by producing the product in the foreign market, even if there are no import barriers—for example, the ability to meet the demand for the product quickly, good public relations with customers and host government, and improved service. Moreover, local production often allows the company to take advantage of incentives that the host government may be offering to foreign companies that make direct investments in the country—such as, reduced taxes for several years, free land, low-interest loans, and a guarantee of no labor strife.

The need for vertical integration is another reason often responsible for the multinationalization of operations. Companies are pushed into making direct investments abroad so that they can capture a source of supply or new markets for their products. For example, a company in the oil exploration and drilling business may integrate "downstream" by acquiring or building an oil refinery in a foreign country that has a market for its refined products. Conversely, a company that has strong distribution channels (gas stations) in a country but which needs a steady source of supply of gasoline at predictable prices may integrate "upstream" and acquire an oil producer and refiner in another country.

Yet another reason for multinationalization of company operations is to follow the company's major customer abroad. For example, the decision by Volkswagen to build its popular cars in the United States induced many German auto parts makers to establish plants in the United States, too, to produce such parts as window cranks, brake equipment, clutches, and diesel injection devices. The managing director of the English company Metal Box, a maker of containers for canning purposes, had this to say about his company's motives for going abroad:

> The need to preserve food in distant lands for use somewhere else will put demand on cans. . . . Metal Box will go abroad wherever the packagers will go, provided, of course, that there is a packager abroad who will buy cans in sufficient quantity to enable Metal Box to build a plant that is economically feasible.[8]

The small size of the domestic market is the reason given by European companies that have developed multinational structures. Companies based in Switzerland—such as Hoffman La-Roche, Sandoz, and Ciba-Geigy—a nation whose population is only about 6 million, could not have survived in their industry had they limited their business horizons to only the Swiss market. These companies, and others like them, were forced to seek markets abroad, which eventually led to the creation of foreign manufacturing facilities in their major markets.

Companies in pharmaceutical and high-technology industries that must spend large sums of money on research and development for new products and processes are compelled to look for ways to improve their sales volume in order to support their laboratories. If the domestic sales volume and exports do not raise the necessary cash flow, then strategically located manufacturing and sales affiliates are established abroad with the objective of attaining higher levels of sales volume and cash flow.

A large number of companies have established production facilities abroad to exploit the strong brand name of their products. Realizing that they could not fully exploit their advantage by way of exports, they have set up plants in their major foreign markets. Examples of companies that have used this strategy are Coca Cola, Heinz, Corn Products, and Del Monte.

SUMMARY

The purpose of this chapter was to provide an introduction to international management and to the world of the so-called international or multinational enterprise. The nature of international business was explained first, and we saw that the need for international management and managers arises when companies begin to export goods or services.

Although there are scores of small multinational companies, generally when one speaks about them the reference is to the large multinationals. Increasingly people are referring to these giant companies, with operations throughout the world, not as international but as multinational companies. International management and multinational companies are more or less like Siamese twins or two sides of a coin. The growth of multinational companies has resulted from the astute management of these enterprises by international managers. And the management of multinational corporations epitomizes what international management is all about.

We saw something of the dimensions and dramatic growth of multinational companies during the 1960s, which was followed by a description of the nature of the international environment in which international management activities occur. Next we looked at the different international business activities of multinational companies, then examined the typical stages in the evolution of multinational companies. An overview of the different reasons for international production by multinational companies completed the chapter.

QUESTIONS

1. What is international business? How does it differ from international management?

2. Discuss the characteristics of multinational companies. What forces have contributed to their development and growth?

3. How does a domestic company typically evolve into one that is multinational? How and why does change occur in the relationship between the parent company and foreign affiliates as the company becomes multinational?

FURTHER READING

1. Daniels, John D.; Ogram, Earnest W., Jr.; and Radebaugh, Lee H. *International Business: Environments and Operations*, 2d ed. Reading, Mass.: Addison-Wesley, 1979.

1. An Introduction to International Management

2. Farmer, Richard N., and Richman, Barry B. *International Business, An Operational Theory.* Homewood, Ill.: Richard D. Irwin, 1966.
3. Fayerweather, John. *International Business Strategy and Administration.* Cambridge, Mass.: Ballinger, 1978.
4. Phatak, Arvind V. *Evolution of World Enterprises.* New York: American Management Association, 1971.
5. Phatak, Arvind. *Managing Multinational Corporations.* New York: Praeger Publishers, 1974.
6. Vernon, Raymond, and Wells, Louis T., Jr. *Manager in the International Economy,* 4th ed. Englewood Cliffs, N.J.: Prentice-Hall, 1981.

NOTES

1. U.S. Department of Commerce, *Survey of Current Business* (Washington, D.C.: U.S. Government Printing Office, August 1979), Table 3, p. 56.
2. U.S. Department of Commerce, *Statistical Abstract of the United States* (Washington, D.C.: U.S. Government Printing Office, 1979), p. 895.
3. John Fayerweather, *International Business Strategy and Administration* (Cambridge, Mass.: Ballinger Publishing Co., 1978), p. 3.
4. John D. Daniels, Earnest W. Ogram, Jr., and Lee H. Radebaugh, *International Business: Environments and Operations,* 2d ed. (Reading, Mass.: Addison-Wesley Publishing Co., 1979), p. 3.
5. Richard N. Farmer and Barry M. Richman, *International Business, An Operational Theory* (Homewood, Ill.: Richard D. Irwin, 1966), p. 13
6. Raymond Vernon and Louis T. Wells, Jr., *Manager in the International Economy,* 4th ed. (Englewood Cliffs, N.J.: Prentice-Hall, 1981), p. 4.
7. For a detailed account of licensing and its advantages and disadvantages, see Arvind Phatak, *Managing Multinational Corporations* (New York: Praeger Publishers, 1974), pp. 276–88.
8. Arvind V. Phatak, *Evolution of World Enterprises* (New York: American Management Association, 1971), p. 37.

Chapter **2**

The Cultural Environment of International Management

The multinational operations of companies have brought executives in face-to-face contact with the cultures of different nations and regions, many of which seem very strange. The importance of understanding the cultures of countries in which a company operates—as well as the similarities and differences between those cultures—becomes clear when one looks at the multitude of blunders international executives have made because of insensitivity to cultural differences.[1] Investigators who have studied the performance and problems of corporations and individuals abroad have concluded that it is usually the human problems associated with working in a different culture that are likely to be critical in the success or failure of their endeavors.[2] Analyses of problems and failures abroad have shown that the techniques, practices, and methods that have proved effective in one country may not work as well in other countries; one dominant interfering factor is culture.

The following old oriental story vividly dramatizes the consequences of ignorance, and it is an appropriate metaphor for the kinds of problems that can arise when people of diverse cultures come into contact without preparation:

Once upon a time there was a great flood, and involved in this flood were two creatures, a monkey and a fish. The monkey, being agile and experienced, was lucky enough to scramble up a tree and escape the raging waters. As he looked down from his safe perch, he saw the poor fish struggling against the swift current. With the very best of intentions, he reached down and lifted the fish from the water. The result was inevitable.[3]

Just as the monkey in the story assumed that the fish's environment was similar to his and behaved accordingly, so do many international executives unconsciously assume that all people think and feel the way they do. Management practices that are suited for their own cultural environment may bring about undesirable, perhaps terrible, consequences in another culture. In international business dealings, then, ignorance of cultural differences is not just unfortunate—it is bad business.

To avoid such problems, the international manager must understand his or her own culture first. A person's behavior is based on a commonly shared cultural system of values, beliefs, and attitudes of the society. When the international manager fully comprehends his or her own culture, as well as that of the country into which the business plans to expand, the manager can be certain of not unconsciously expecting the foreign nationals to behave like the "normal" people of her or his own culture. The manager must recognize the cultural imperatives abroad, making appropriate changes in his or her own interpersonal behavior and managerial practices.

In this chapter we shall examine the concept of culture and value orientations that are typical of American and most Western societies. We shall study how these value orientations differ from those of non-Western societies and problems that occur when the diverse Western and non-Western value orientations interact with each other when people from these cultures come face to face.

A manager living abroad needs a framework in which to analyze and understand the differences between her or his own culture and that of the host society. We shall look at one such scheme for evaluating cultural differences.

THE MEANING OF CULTURE

There are as many definitions of culture as there are books in anthropology. Culture is the way of life of a group of people. It is "that complex whole which includes knowledge, belief, art, morals, customs, and any other capabilities and habits acquired by man as a member of society."[4] In other words, it is the distinctive way of life of a group of people, their complete design for living.[5] A person is not born with a given culture; rather she or he acquires it through the socialization process that begins at birth: an American is not born with a liking for hot dogs, or a German with a natural preference for beer; these behavioral attributes are culturally transmitted.

Dressler and Carns list the following characteristics of culture quoted below:

1. Culture exists in the minds of individual human beings who have learned it in their past associations with other human beings and who use it to guide their own continuing interaction with others.

2. Human cultures vary considerably, one from another.

3. But although different in some respects, cultures resemble one another to a considerable extent.

4. Once a culture has been learned and accepted, it tends to persist.

5. All cultures are gradually and continuously being changed, even though human beings tend to resist these changes.

6. Different individuals of the same society may behave differently in response to a given situation, even though all have internalized certain elements of the same culture.

7. No person can escape entirely from his culture.[6]

Dressler and Carns offer the following as the functions of culture:

1. Culture enables us to communicate with others through a language that we have learned and that we share in common

2. Culture makes it possible to anticipate how others in our society are likely to respond to our actions

3. Culture gives us standards for distinguishing between what is considered right or wrong, beautiful and ugly, reasonable and unreasonable, tragic and humorous, safe and dangerous

4. Culture provides the knowledge and skill necessary for meeting sustenance needs

5. Culture enables us to identify with—that is, include ourselves in the same category with—other people of similar background.[7]

VALUES CRITICAL TO INTERNATIONAL MANAGEMENT EFFECTIVENESS

The nature of all the problems encountered by international managers abroad may be perceived as this: a conflict between the basic values held by two or more groups of people. The problems and misunderstandings occur because of the ethnocentric attitudes of members of each group, who take for granted that their values, especially those that tend to be acted on unconsciously, are correct and indeed best. In the following section, we shall identify and discuss some specific values held by Americans which frequently are at odds with those of people of other cultures. These values may not be characteristic of all Americans—after all, America is considered the melting pot of many different cultures and nationalities—but they do represent values common to many Americans and tend to distinguish the U.S. culture from other contemporary cultures.

Individualism

Individualism describes the attitude of independence of the person who feels a large degree of freedom in the conduct of his or her personal life. In the American culture, this individualism may motivate personal accomplishment and self-expression is considered to be of the greatest worth. By contrast, individualism is not considered important in other cultures. In the Chinese culture, the group is preeminent in social life, so conformity and cooperation are values that rank higher than individualism. Individual successes or failures are shared by the family, clan, or community.

Informality

The American culture is not one that attaches a great deal of importance to tradition, ceremony, and social rules. This informality has caused serious problems for businesses operating in other cultures. Latin American countries, for example, are extreme cases of the formal society. The Latin American likes pomp and circumstance and is quite at ease with it. He or she likes lavish public receptions and processions and would expect that an outsider would carefully observe all amenities of personal etiquette and hospitality. An American, when immersed in a culture like this, is likely to feel ill at ease; she or he must take special precautions to avoid appearing blatantly casual and informal in words and deeds in order to not offend the Latin hosts.

Another value related to informality is the American inclination to not "beat around the bush"—to get to the point of the matter in business meetings and conversations. In Saudi Arabia or Latin American countries, however, it is customary to converse first about unrelated matters before embarking on the business discussions for which the meeting was arranged. An American should realize that people of other cultures often feel it is important to get to know one another and develop mutual trust before getting down to business negotiations or problems. Barging straight into the business issue, without the informal small talk at the beginning, may make a Saudi Arabian or Latin American so uncomfortable that the American who insists on such an approach may very well not get what he or she came for.

Materialism

The United States has been blessed with abundant natural resources, a fact which seems to have made Americans—in the eyes of foreigners—wasteful in their consumption of both resources and material goods. Visiting foreigners are often astonished to see cars less than ten years old heaped in junkyards. These cars would probably still be on the road in most countries because other cultures seem more inclined to foster an awareness of the need for conserving resources and preserving material goods. The more wasteful American attitude has been said to arise from the American Frontier philosophy—that humans are the masters of nature and should therefore conquer, change, and control nature for the benefit of humankind. This philosophy is at total variance with the philosophies of the peoples of India, Korea, and Egypt, for example. In India and Korea worship of nature is part of the religious dogma. And even for persons for whom religion is not the significant determinant of behavior, the river Ganges in India and the Nile in Egypt are revered for their power over the economic and physical well-being of the people. An American must strive to be aware of the differences between her or his own attitude toward nature and those of other cultures; all of us should be careful not to judge other cultures on the basis of the quality or quantity of physical goods present in daily life.

There is also a tendency in Western cultures to attach status to certain physical objects—such as a suit made by a famous clothing manufacturer, or a recent model car. Many non-Western cultures foster no interest in acquiring such symbols; rather, the emphasis is on finding and enjoying aesthetic and spiritual values. An understanding of these differences in values is important for the international manager because behavior that may seem strange to an American may be the necessary expression of fundamental values held by the person from a different culture.

Change

Societies differ in their attitudes toward change and progress. Although change is inevitable, non-Western people look upon change as a phenomenon that occurs naturally and as part of the overall evolution of humans and their universe. Change in such societies is accepted, but passively, without any deliberate effort to bring it about. The people in Western societies, however, feel that the future is not predestined and that humans, by actions and deeds, are capable of manipulating the environment in which they shall live in the future and can change it to their liking.

These differences in attitudes towards change may account for the often fatalistic attitude of non-Western people; the passivity may be partially responsible for the difficulties encountered by Western managers and technicians in introducing innovations in non-Western societies.

Time Orientation

Time can be considered a communication system, just as words or languages are. Like different spoken languages, the languages of time are also different. These so-called unspoken languages "are informal, yet the rules governing their interpretation are surprisingly ironbound."[8]

Western cultures, and particularly the American, perceive time as a resource—and an extremely scarce one—that is continuously depleting. Americans, therefore, emphasize the efficient use of time. Terms such as "time is money," "time never comes back," and "time is the enemy," are often used to promote the effective use of time. This orientation is due to the Western belief that there is a limited amount of total time available to a person—that which he or she has from birth to death—and therefore one should make the most of it. This perception of time has made Americans conscious of the need for establishing deadlines for work to be done and to stick to them. It also accounts for Americans being very fastidious about making and keeping appointments.

In contrast Eastern cultures view time as an unlimited and unending resource. For a Hindu, time does not begin at birth or end at death. Belief in reincarnation gives life a nontemporal dimension and hence time is perceived to be an inexhaustible resource. This attitude towards time makes people in Eastern cultures quite casual about keeping appointments and deadlines, an indifference which makes Americans dealing with them very anxious and frustrated.

The rather cavalier Eastern attitude toward time is illustrated in the following incident:

> In comparing the United States with Iran and Afghanistan very great differences in the handling of time appear. The American attitude toward appointments is an example. Once while in Tehran I had an opportunity to observe some young Iranians making plans for a party. After plans were made to pick up everyone at appointed times and places everything began to fall apart. People would leave messages that they were unable to take so-and-so or were going somewhere else, knowing full well that the person who had been given the message couldn't possibly deliver it. One girl was left stranded on a street corner, and no one seemed to be concerned about it. One of my informants explained that he himself had many similar experiences. Once he had made eleven appointments to see a friend. Each time one of them failed to show up. The twelfth time they swore they would both be there, that nothing would interfere. The friend failed to arrive. After waiting for forty-five minutes my informant phoned his friend and found him still at home. The following conversation is an approximation of what took place:
> "Is that you, Abdul?" "Yes." "Why aren't you here? I thought we were to meet for sure." "Oh, but it was raining," said Abdul with a sort of whining intonation."[9]

In the United States the time spent waiting outside a person's office beyond the appointed time is seen as a measure of the importance of the person kept waiting. Americans therefore get very upset if they are kept waiting for thirty minutes or more and consider this to be a personal affront. In the Middle East there is no such interpretation: a businessperson may keep a visitor waiting for a long time; but once the businessperson does see the visitor, the interview will last as long as may be necessary to complete the business at hand—but this approach means that the businessperson is likely to keep the next visitor waiting for hours too.

There are many more value orientations along which the American and Western cultures differ from non-Western cultures. The scope of this chapter does not permit the discussion of every one of them. However, the purpose of the preceding discussion of value orientations was to point out that differences in behavior are due to differences in the value orientations of societies.

PROBLEMS CAUSED BY CULTURAL DIFFERENCES

We have seen that the international manager can face, or cause, many problems in a foreign host country because of cultural differences. This section gives a few examples of problems created by cultural insensitivity:

> Some years ago, in 1946, an agricultural extension worker introduced a new type of hybrid maize into a community of Spanish American farmers in New Mexico. He was already well known and liked. He was able to demonstrate that the new seed yielded three times as much as the seed the farmers normally planted, and he was certain that he was doing right in persuading them to grow it. They followed his advice, but within three years they had nearly all gone back to growing their old low-yielding variety.
>
> This sounds almost incredible, but it can be explained quite simply. The farmers ate the maize they grew. They ground it into flour and with the flour their wives made tortillas—the flat round cakes that formed the staple of their diet. But the new type of maize gave a flavour to the cakes the people did not like. The people valued the high yield but did not like the price they had to pay in taste, and the innovation failed because the agency had overlooked the need to test for taste as well as yield before the seed was given to the farmers.[10]

The preceding example shows the influence of cultural preferences—and the difficulties we can encounter if we assume that others have the same tastes as we do or the same priorities.

The following incident shows the impact of the differences in time orientation. In Western societies, one could suffer severe penalties for not completing work on time—and enjoy significant rewards for meeting work schedules and deadlines. The Western worker feels that he or she is duty bound to keep promises and believes that his or her reputation will be tarnished for failure to deliver on time. When two persons involved in a business transaction have two totally opposite orientations towards time schedules, a lot of difficulty will result; the following is an example:

> The Middle Eastern peoples are a case in point. Not only is our idea of time schedules no part of Arab life but the mere mention of a deadline to an Arab is like waving a red flag in front of a bull. In his culture, your emphasis on a deadline has the emotional effect on him that his backing you into a corner and threatening you with a club would have on you.
>
> One effect of this conflict of unconscious habit patterns is that hundreds of American-owned radio sets are lying on the shelves of Arab radio repair shops, untouched. The Americans made the serious cross-cultural error of asking to have the repair completed by a certain time.
>
> How do you cope with this? How does the Arab get another Arab to do anything? Every culture has its own ways of bringing pressure to get results. The usual Arab way is one which Americans avoid as "bad manners." It is needling.
>
> An Arab businessman whose car broke down explained it this way:
>
> > First, I go the garage and tell the mechanic what is wrong with my car. I wouldn't want to give him the idea that I didn't know. After that, I leave the car and walk around the block. When I come back to the garage, I ask him if he has started to work yet. On my way home for lunch I stop in and ask him how things are going. When I go back to the office I stop by again. In the evening, I return and peer over his shoulder for awhile. If I didn't keep this up, he'd be off working on someone else's car.
> >
> > If you haven't been needled by an Arab, you just haven't been needled.[11]

Language can also pose a problem for international managers. And the problem with language is not just with having to learn a new vocabulary. Many international managers have learned from experience that one word or idiom may have a different meaning and implication in another culture that uses the same language. For instance, in England the word *homely* means friendly, warm, and comfortable; in the United States it means plain, or even ugly. Similarly, the phrase *come any time* can have different interpretations:

> Visiting time involves the question of who sets the time for a visit. George Coelho, a social psychologist from India, gives an illustrative case. A U.S. businessman received this invitation from an Indian businessman: "Won't you and your family come and see us? Come anytime." Several weeks later, the Indian repeated the invitation in the same words. Each time the American replied that he would certainly like to drop in—but he never did. The reason is obvious in terms of our culture. Here "come any time" is just an expression of friendliness. You are not really expected to show up unless your host proposes a specific time. In India, on the contrary, the words are meant literally—that the host is putting himself at the disposal of his guest and really expects him to come. It is the essence of politeness to leave it to the guest to set a time at his convenience. If the guest never comes, the Indian naturally assumes that he does not want to come. Such a misunderstanding can lead to a serious rift between men who are trying to do business with each other.[12]

In the American culture it is generally expected that when a manager asks her or his subordinate if a task could be completed by a certain date, the latter would say *yes* or *no* and give the reasons why if the answer is *no*. But once the subordinate has agreed to complete the task on time, he or she is expected to abide by the promise. Western society emphasizes the value of truthfulness in interpersonal behavior.

However, in Japan or India a person is likely to make a promise to do something while knowing quite well that it cannot be kept. The reluctance to say *no* to a request is due to the person's reluctance to displease someone with a negative answer, and also to save the embarrassment of having to admit that one is incapable of doing what he or she has been asked to do. The following incident illustrates this phenomenon and the problem that it can create for a Western businessperson:

> An American businessman would be most unlikely to question another businessman's word if he were technically qualified and said that his plant could produce 1000 gross of widgets a month. We are "taught" that it is none of our business to inquire too deeply into the details of his production system. This would be prying and might be considered an attempt to steal his operational plans.

> Yet this cultural pattern has trapped many an American into believing that when a Japanese manufacturer answered a direct question with the

reply that he could produce 1000 gross of widgets, he meant what he said. If the American had been escorted through the factory and saw quite clearly that its capacity was, at the most, perhaps 500 gross of widgets per month, he would be likely to say to himself: "Well, this fellow probably has a brother-in-law. Besides, what business is it of mine, so long as he meets the schedule?"

The cables begin to burn after the American returns home and only 500 gross of widgets arrive each month. What the American did not know was that in Japanese culture one avoids the direct question unless the questioner is absolutely certain that the answer will not embarrass the Japanese businessman in any way whatsoever. In Japan for one to admit being unable to perform a given operation or measure up to a given standard means a bitter loss of face. Given a foreigner who is so stupid, ignorant, or insensitive as to ask an embarrassing question, the Japanese is likely to choose what appears to him the lesser of two evils.

Americans caught in this cross-cultural communications trap are apt to feel doubly deceived because the Japanese manufacturer may well be an established and respected member of the business community.[13]

ANALYZING CULTURAL DIFFERENCES

An international manager needs a conceptual scheme to analyze cultural differences between his native culture and the foreign culture. An approach that may be useful is to identify the various dimensions of culture along which cultural differences could be measured. One such scheme is that which has been developed by Herskovits.[14] He lists five dimensions of culture.

1. Material culture
2. Social Institutions
3. Man and Universe
4. Aesthetics
5. Language

Material Culture

Material culture affects the level of demand for goods and the quality and types of products demanded. It is composed of two aspects: technology and economics. *Technology* refers to the techniques used to produce material goods, as well as the technical know-how of a country. *Economics* can be described as the manner in which a culture makes use of its capabilities and the resulting benefits. The multinational company involved in selling electrical appliances, for example, should analyze the material culture of the proposed foreign market. For instance, a firm may be able to sell microwave ovens in England and France but will find few buyers in New Guinea. It would be good to be able to anticipate that outcome by understanding the material cultures of the three nations.

Social Institutions

Social institutions—whether they be of a business, political, family, or social class nature—influence the behavior of individuals. An American in Japan, for example, must recognize that there social institutions favor a paternalistic leadership style and decision making that is by nature participative and consensus oriented. In India, a fair amount of nepotism is a feature of the joint-family system.

Man and the Universe

This dimension is composed of elements such as religion and superstitions, both of which have a profound impact on the value and belief systems of individuals. Making light of superstitions when doing business with other cultures may prove to be an expensive mistake. In parts of Asia, for example, ghosts, fortune telling, palmistry and soothsayers are all integral parts of culture and must be understood as influential in peoples' lives and in business dealings as well.

Aesthetics

This includes the art, folklore, music, and drama of a culture. The aesthetics of a particular culture can be important in the interpretation of symbolic meanings of various artistic expressions. Failure to correctly interpret symbolic values can be problematic for multinational companies. For instance, in India, folklore has established the owl as a symbol of bad luck, so clearly the owl should not be used in advertising.

Language

Of all the cultural elements that an international manager must study, language is probably the most difficult. One needs more than the ability to speak a language, one also needs the competancy to recognize idiomatic interpretations, which are quite different from those found in the dictionary. Thus the international manager can not take for granted that he or she is always communicating effectively in another language. Small nuances of the local tongue may elude a foreigner who has not been immersed in the foreign culture for a long time.

To the preceding list of Herskovits we could add one more category— *religion*. We saw that religion can reasonably be considered to be a part of the Man and the Universe dimension; but it could well be a dimension by itself, especially in cultures in which religion is a central, organizational feature. Religion in such societies has a profound effect on how business is conducted. For example, consumption of pork is forbidden by Islam and Judaism. In Christian societies Sunday is the day of rest, whereas in Islamic countries it is Friday, and in Israel it is Saturday. Islam forbids "excessive" profit, which is considered to be a form of exploitation. Islam preaches moderation and the sharing of wealth with others less fortunate, so individuals are held accountable for the well-being of the community. The concept of sharing wealth is manifested in one form called *zakat*, which is an annual tax of 2.5 percent collected from individuals and used for the benefit of the community. Islam also forbids usury; hence, banks in fundamentalist Islamic nations take equity in financing ventures, sharing profits as well as losses in the joint venture.

The impact of fundamentalist Islamic concepts and culture on marketing in Islamic countries is so significant that it is worthwhile to look at it in greater detail. Exhibit 2-1 shows how some elements of the institutionalized Islam religion affect international marketing.

SUMMARY

In this chapter we focused on the cultural environment of international management. Culture was defined as "that complex whole which includes knowledge, belief, art, morals, customs, and any other capabilities and habits acquired by man as a member of society." It has been

EXHIBIT 2-1 *Marketing in an Islamic Culture*

Elements	*Implications for Marketing*
Fundamental Islamic Concepts	
Unity. (Concept of centrality, oneness of God, harmony in life.)	Product standardization; mass techniques; central balance; unity in advertising copy and layout; strong brand loyalities; a smaller evoked size set; loyalty to company; opportunities for brand-extension strategies.
Legitimacy. (Fair dealings, reasonable level of profits.)	Less need for formal product warranties, greater need for institutional advertising and advocacy advertising, especially by foreign firms; a switch from profit maximizing to a profit satisfying strategy.
Zakaat. (2.5 percent per annum compulsory tax binding on all classified as "not poor.")	Use of "excessive" profits, if any, for charitable acts; corporate donations for charity; institutional advertising.
Usury. (Cannot charge interest on loans. A general interpretation of this law defines "excessive interest" charged on loans as not permissible.)	Avoid direct use of credit as a marketing tool; establish a consumer policy of paying cash for low-value products; for high-value products offer discounts for cash payments and raise prices of products on an installment basis; sometimes possible to conduct interest transactions between local/foreign firm in other non-Islamic countries; banks in some Islamic countries take equity in financing ventures, sharing resultant profits (and losses).
Supremacy of human life. (Compared to other forms of life and to objects, human life is of supreme importance.)	Pet food and products are less important; avoid use of statues and busts, which are interpreted as objects of idolatry; symbols in advertising and promotion should reflect high human values; use floral designs and artwork in advertising as representation of aesthetic values.

Community.
(All Muslims should strive to achieve universal brotherhood—with allegiance to the "one God." One way of expressing community is the required (if at all possible) pilgrimmage to Mecca for all Muslims, at least once in their lifetime.

Development of an "Islamic consumer," who is served with Islam-oriented products and services—for example, "kosher" meat packages, gifts exchanged at Muslim festivals, and so forth; development of community services: train persons in marketing or nonprofit organizations and skills.

Equality of peoples.

Abstinence.
(During the month of Ramadan, Muslims are required to fast without food or drink from the first streak of dawn to sunset—as a reminder to those who are more fortunate to be kind to the less fortunate and as an exercise in self-control.)

A participative communication system exists in Islam, especially with regard to abstinence: roles and authority structures may be rigidly defined but accessibility at any level is relatively easy. Market possibilities: products that are nutritious, cool, and digested easily can be formulated for Sehr and Iftar (beginning and end of the fast).

Consumption of alcohol and pork is forbidden, as is gambling.

Opportunities for developing nonalcoholic items and beverages (for example, soft drinks, ice cream, milk shakes, fruit juices) and nonchance social games, such as Scrabble; food products should use vegetable or beef shortening.

(cont.)

EXHIBIT 2-1 *(cont.)*

Elements	Implications for Marketing
Fundamental Islamic Concepts	
Environmentalism (The universe created by God was pure. Consequently, the land, air, and water should be held as sacred elements.)	Anticipate environmental, antipollution laws; opportunities for companies involved in maintaining a clean environment; easier acceptance of pollution-control devices in the community (for example, recent efforts in Turkey have been well received by the local communities.)
Worship (Five times a day; timing of prayers varies.)	Need to take into account the variability and shift in prayer timings in planning sales calls, work schedules, business hours, customer traffic, and so forth.
Elements of Islamic culture	
Obligation to family and tribal traditions.	Importance of respected members in the family or tribe as opinion leaders; word-of-mouth communication, as well as customer referrals, may be critical; social or clan allegiances, affiliations, and associations may be possible surrogates for reference groups; advertising home-oriented products stressing family roles may be highly effective—for example, electronic games.
Obligation to parents is sacred.	Enhance the image of functional products with advertisements that stress parental advice or approval; even with children's products, there should be less emphasis on children as decision makers.

Obligation to extend hospitality to both insiders and outsiders.	Product designs that are symbols of hospitality, outwardly open in expression; rate of new product acceptance may be accelerated and eased by appeals based on community.
Obligations to conform to codes of sexual conduct and social interaction. These may include the following:	
1. Modest dress for women in public.	More colorful clothing and accessories are worn by women at home, so promotion of products for use in private homes could be more intimate—such audiences could be reached effectively through women's magazines; avoid use of immodest exposure and sexual implications in public settings.
2. Separation of male and female audiences (in some cases).	Access to female consumers can often be gained only through women as selling agents, salespersons, catalogs, home demonstrations, and women's specialty shops.
Obligations to observe religious occasions. (For example, there are two major religious observances that are celebrated: Eid-ul-Fitr, Eid-ul-Adha.)	Purchase likely for these occasions—new shoes, clothing, sweets, and preparation of food items for family reunions, Muslim gatherings; there has been a practice of giving money in place of gifts; increasingly, however, a shift is taking place to more gift giving; owing to use of lunar calendar, dates are not fixed.

SOURCE: Adapted from Mushtaq Luqmani, Zahir A. Quraeshi, and Linda Delene, "Marketing in Islamic Countries: A Viewpoint," *MSU Business Topics*, Summer 1980, pp. 20–21.

emphasized throughout the chapter that most problems that managers living abroad face are those arising from conflicts between the value orientations of different cultures.

Some specific values held by Americans which frequently conflict with those of peoples of other cultures were discussed: individualism, informality, materialism, attitude toward change, and orientation toward the concept of time. Next, we looked at several illustrations of problems caused by cultural differences. Finally, we considered a conceptual scheme for analyzing cultural differences.

QUESTIONS

1. Why should an international executive understand cultural differences?

2. Even though the U.S. has been described as a "melting pot," are there any significant differences in the observed behavior of ethnic groups (Italian, Irish, Polish, German) that can be attributed to cultural differences?

FURTHER READING

1. Adams, Dan. "The Monkey and the Fish: Cultural Pitfalls of an Educational Advisor." *International Development Review*, 2, no. 2 (1969).

2. Arensberg, Conrad M., and Niehoff, Arthur H. *Introducing Social Change: A Manual for Americans Overseas.* Chicago: Aldine, 1964.

3. Batten, Thomas R. *Communities and Their Development.* New York: Oxford University Press, 1957.

4. Cleveland, Harlan; Mangone, Gerard J.; Adams, John C. *The Overseas Americans.* New York: McGraw-Hill, 1960.

5. Dressler, David, and Carns, Donald. *Sociology, the Study of Human Interactions.* New York: Alfred A. Knopf, 1969.

6. Fayerweather, John. *The Executive Overseas.* Syracuse: Syracuse University Press, 1959.

7. Foster, George M. *Traditional Cultures: And the Impact of Technological Change.* New York: Harper & Brothers, 1962.

8. Hall, Edward T. "The Silent Language in Overseas Business." *Harvard Business Review*, May–June 1960.

9. Hall, Edward T. *The Silent Language*. Garden City, N. Y.: Anchor Press/Doubleday, Anchor Books Edition, 1973.

10. Hall, Edward T., and Whyte, William F. "Intercultural Communication: A Guide to Men of Action." *Human Organization* 19, no. 1 (Spring 1960).

11. Herskovits, Melville J. *Man and His Works*. New York: Alfred A. Knopf, 1954.

12. Lerner, Daniel, and Lasswell, Harold D., eds. *The Policy Sciences*. Stanford: Stanford University Press, 1951.

13. Lugmani, Mushtag; Quraeshi, Zahir A.; and Delene, Linda. "Marketing in Islamic Countries: A Viewpoint." *MSU Business Topics*, Summer 1980.

14. Montgomery, John D. "Crossing the Culture Bars; An Approach to the Training of American Technicians for Overseas Assignments." *World Politics* 13, no. 4 (July 1961).

15. Ricks, David; Fu, Marilyn Y. C.; and Arpan, Jeffrey S. *International Business Blunders*. Columbus, Ohio: Grid, 1974.

16. Terpstra, Vern. *The Cultural Environment of International Business*. Cincinnati: South-Western Publishing Company, 1978.

NOTES

1. For an excellent documentation of incidents illustrating such blunders, see David Ricks, Marilyn Y. C. Fu, and Jeffrey S. Arpan, *International Business Blunders* (Columbus, Ohio: Grid, Inc., 1974).

2. See, for example, Harlan Cleveland, Gerard J. Mangone, and John Clarke Adams, *The Overseas Americans* (New York: McGraw-Hill Book Co., 1960); John D. Montgomery, "Crossing the Culture Bars: An Approach to the Training of American Technicians for Overseas Assignments," *World Politics* 13, no. 4 (July 1961): 544–60; George M. Foster, *Traditional Cultures: And the Impact of Technological Change* (New York: Harper and Brothers, 1962); John Fayerweather, *The Executive Overseas* (Syracuse: Syracuse University Press, 1959); and Conrad M. Arensberg and Arther H. Niehoff, *Introducing Social Change: A Manual for Americans Overseas* (Chicago: Aldine Publishing Co.), 1964.

3. Don Adams, "The Monkey and the Fish: Cultural Pitfalls of an Educational Advisor," *International Development Review* 2, no. 2 (1969): 22.

4. Melville J. Herskovits, *Man and His Works* (New York: Alfred A. Knopf, 1952), p. 17.

5. Clyde Kluckhohn, "The Study of Culture," in *The Policy Sciences*, ed. Daniel Lerner and Harold D. Lasswell (Stanford: Stanford University Press, 1951), p. 86.

6. David Dressler and Donald Carns, *Sociology, The Study of Human Interaction* (New York: Alfred A. Knopf, 1969), pp. 56–59.
7. Ibid., p. 60.
8. Edward T. Hall, "The Silent Language in Overseas Business," *Harvard Business Review*, May–June 1960, p. 138.
9. Edward T. Hall, *The Silent Language* (Garden City, N.Y.: Anchor Press/Doubleday, Anchor Books Edition, 1973), p. 18. Copyright © 1959 by Edward T. Hall. Reprinted by permission of Doubleday & Company, Inc.
10. Thomas R. Batten, *Communities and their Development* (New York: Oxford University Press, 1957), pp. 10–11. Reprinted by permission.
11. Edward T. Hall and William Foote Whyte, "Intercultural Communications: A Guide to Men of Action," *Human Organization* 19, no. 1 (Spring 1960): 9. Reproduced by permission of the Society for Applied Anthropology from *Human Organization*.
12. Ibid. pp. 8–9.
13. Ibid. pp. 6–7.
14. Herskovits, *Man and His Works*. p. 17.

Chapter **3**

Planning in
an International Setting

This chapter is about the planning function in an international setting. The international setting is complex; hence the problems and issues confronting international planning are equally complex. Lack of planning would almost certainly result in misallocation of resources and a disappointing performance of the company's global operation. But a well-designed international corporate strategy allows a company to set realistic objectives and to deploy and use its resources efficiently on a global scale.

The focus of this chapter is on planning at the parent company level of an international company. At the core of this presentation are the issues that the top management at headquarters have to come to grips with in developing strategies for the company's international involvement.

WHAT IS PLANNING?

Planning is one of the basic functions in the management process. Every manager must have plans so as to reach maximum organizational effectiveness. Planning involves the assessment of the environment for opportunities and threats of the foreseeable future, evaluation of the strengths and weaknesses of the enterprise, and the formulation of objectives and strategies designed to exploit the opportunities and combat the threats.

All planning is concerned with the future; it is concerned with deciding what an enterprise wants to be and wants to achieve—how to attain these aspirations, allocate resources, and implement designs.

Russel L. Ackoff says that "planning is the design of a desired future and of effective ways of bringing it about."[1] He goes on to say that "planning is a process that involves making and evaluating each of a set of interrelated decisions before action is required, in a situation in which it is believed that unless action is taken a desired future state is not likely to occur, and that, if appropriate action is taken, the likelihood of a favorable outcome can be increased."[2] To George A. Steiner, "planning deals with the futurity of present decisions."[3] This, he says, can mean one of two things—or both. "Planning examines future alternative courses of action which are open to a company. In choosing from among these courses of action an umbrella, a perspective, a frame of reference is established for current decisions. Also it can mean that planning examines the evolving chains of cause and effect likely to result from current decisions."[4]

WHAT IS INTERNATIONAL PLANNING?

All the aspects of planning just mentioned are applicable to international planning as well. In addition, international planning is concerned with the assessment of the multinational environment, determining the future worldwide opportunities and threats, and formulating the global objectives and strategies of the enterprise in light of this environmental assessment and the internal audit of the enterprise's strengths and weaknesses. International planning includes the formulation of short- and long-term goals and objectives, and the allocation of resources—people, capital, technology, information—internationally to achieve the enterprise's global aims.

THE ENVIRONMENT
OF INTERNATIONAL PLANNING

Planning in an international company is far more complicated than in a company that does not operate internationally. What makes it difficult is the complexity of the international environment. A domestic company—one that operates in the market of a single country—is required to monitor basically only the environment of one country, although it should also keep an eye on developments in other countries that may have an impact on its domestic environment. In an international company, a manager must monitor not only the changes in the environments of every country in which the company currently has operations, but also how these environments are likely to affect one another, as well as how the changes occurring in the global environment will affect the manager's domain.

Important Environmental Issues and Problems

Global planning evolves in response to two sets of environmental forces—changes in the external environment, particularly those over which the company management has little or no control, and changes in the internal environment of the company itself. In most companies international planning is still in its infancy, but even the plans that are developed and sophisticated still continue to encounter problems.

We shall first examine the external issues of most concern to international enterprises and the problems they create in the area of international planning. (In the next section, we shall look at internal issues and problems.) Some of the most significant external issues and problems international companies have to confront in their planning of the global operations are listed below.

Political Instability and Risk

Many countries in which international companies have business operations have experienced frequent changes of government as well as unexpected modifications of a government's economic policies. Changes in government policies toward the industrial and commercial sector of the economy and particularly toward foreign firms, foreign trade, and foreign investment have had significant impact on the profits and other goals of international firms.

Currency Instability

Fluctuations in the exchange rates of currencies—especially those involving the U.S. dollar, the British pound, the German mark, the Swiss franc, and the Japanese yen—have been responsible for wild swings in the financial standing of many international companies. Some companies such as Exxon have been fortunate enough to have gained as much as $588 million in one year from foreign exchange transactions, whereas others, like Colgate, have lost $13 million or more from such transactions.

Competition from State-owned Enterprises

State-owned (government-owned) enterprises are presenting a growing competitive threat to international companies. State-owned companies—such as Aerospatiale of France, which is in the aerospace industry; Montedison in the chemicals industry, which is 50 percent owned by the Italian government; and VIAG, the state-owned German company, which is in the aluminum industry—are rapidly changing the rules of the game in international competition. These companies are heavily subsidized by their respective governments and are not required to earn profits and returns on investments at levels comparable to those expected of their privately owned competitors.[5]

Pressures from National Governments

International companies have come under severe criticism for their alleged conduct from the foreign governments of both developed and developing countries. They have been accused of such things as disrupting national economic plans, transferring obsolete or inappropriate technology abroad, avoiding taxes by manipulating transfer prices of goods and services, "exporting" jobs by establishing "runaway" plants in low-wage locales, and crushing indigenous competitors with their superior financial and technological power.

Nationalism

The desire for independence among nations, especially the developing ones, has promoted nationalism in many parts of the world. Nationalism does not subscribe to any one particular political ideology: governments having a right-wing political ideology can be just as nationalistic as those with a left-wing philosophy. Regardless of its ideological basis, nationalism does prompt the government to impose restrictive policies against foreign-owned companies—such as import controls, local equity requirements, local content requirements, restrictions on hiring of foreign nationals, limitations on repatriation of profits and dividends, and so on.

Patent and Trademark Protection:

Different countries have different laws for the protection of patents and trademarks. The recent trend in many countries is to reduce or completely abolish such protection granted to the industrial property rights of enterprises. This trend is having a significant impact on research and development and on product planning activities.

Intense Competition

As increasing numbers of companies become active internationally, competition among them for resources and markets is becoming increasingly severe. Until the late 1950s, international companies were predominantly U.S.-based, although there were at that time a few large companies—like Unilever, Royal Dutch Shell, and Nestlé—that were European in origin. Since the early 1960s there has been a mushrooming of international companies based not only in the United States and Europe but also in Japan and in the developing countries such as Taiwan, South Korea, Brazil, and India.

Important Internal Issues and Problems

Multinational companies are continually confronted with several internal issues and problems in international planning. Some of the most significant of these are listed below.

Integrating the Foreign and Domestic Units

An international company can enjoy the benefits of economies of scale in each of the functional areas—production, marketing, finance, purchasing, etc.—if it can effectively coordinate its various foreign and domestic units and make them all work together as one system. To what degree should a company attempt such integration? Should integration of subsidiaries be attempted globally? Or should subsidiaries just in one region—Europe, for example—be grouped for integration purposes? And should all functions be involved in the integration, or merely one or two functions such as production or finance? These are critical issues for the top management of an international company to resolve.

Centralized Control versus Decentralized Initiative

International corporations have a lot to gain from the initiative and drive of the management of their subsidiaries. Subsidiary managers, being close to where the action is in the subsidiary, are often in a better position than those at the parent company to make decisions on the basis of existing circumstances. There are times when decisions must be made on the spot in order to resolve a problem confronting the foreign subsidiary. Moreover, the geographic distance between the parent company and the foreign subsidiary makes decentralized decision making at the subsidiary level almost a necessity. However, some degree of centralization of decision making helps in integrating the foreign subsidiaries, producing benefits that accrue from economies of scale. Top management at the parent company fears the dangers of fragmentation that would befall the multinational company system if each foreign affiliate were allowed to enjoy excessive autonomy. There is, therefore, a basic conflict between centralization and decentralization of authority that top managers at the parent company are obliged to resolve.

The types of questions that parent company managers must answer are: What types of decisions should be made by the parent company? Should alternatives prior to the making of a decision be generated by the parent company, or should they originate from the foreign subsidiary? Are there any areas in which decisions should be made jointly by the parent company and foreign subsidiary managers? Finding answers that are acceptable to all parties and in the best interests of the international company as a whole is a challenge that managers in international companies have to face and handle effectively.

Developing Managers with an International Perspective

International companies need managers at all levels of the organization, parent and subsidiary, who can not only think, plan, and act strategically but do so with a worldwide perspective. For that capacity, a manager should have the knowledge and appreciation of: (1) the differences—cultural, economic, political, sociological, technological, etc.—that exist between the various regions and countries of the world, and of (2) the trends and events occurring, and how rapidly they are occurring, in the world. Having an international perspective also implies an ability and willingness on the part of managers to think and act on a companywide basis. For example, a subsidiary manager in Egypt, if she or he is truly international in orientation, will make decisions that may not be in her or his subsidiary's best interests but which may benefit the entire international company. The loyalty of managers in an international company should be to the company as a whole and not to any one organizational unit within it. How to develop managers with such an international perspective is a problem that top management of international companies must handle effectively.

Internalizing Environmental Information

International companies must search and identify systematically and thoroughly important environmental factors, trends, and events which may have a significant impact on their worldwide operations. This activity is critical and should be conducted on the level of the country, the region, and the whole corporation. In addition, information obtained from such environmental assessments must be used in the development of the company's strategies. Although the importance of environmental assessment and its use in planning is acknowledged by international managers, "most large companies have done a rather poor job of international environmental analysis"[6] and many dismal failures in international operations have been reported because companies did not properly perform the environmental assessment task. Managers are faced with the issue of choosing the best way of obtaining the necessary environmental data, deciding on the type of organization that can provide it most effectively, and ensuring that "the information itself can find its way into planning and decision making on a less haphazard and superficial basis than is often the case."[7]

Worldwide Resource Allocation

An issue that all international planners face involves the allocation of physical, financial, and human resources to old products versus the development of new products, and for the expansion of old country markets versus the development of new country markets. An ideal product/country portfolio would be that which provides the firm with a steady flow of cash for new product and market development and a rate of return on investment that is acceptable to top management. Achieving the proper balance between new and old products, and new and old markets is a challenging task for international planners.

CONSEQUENCES OF LACK OF PLANNING

An international company should have an overall plan and a well-designed strategy for entry into foreign markets. Too many companies have entered foreign markets via licensing, contract manufacturing, or production facilities without a deliberate plan for foreign market penetration, only to find later that the particular strategy chosen was wrong in light of later developments. For example, a company may begin its involvement in a foreign market in the form of export sales in response to inquiries from foreign distributors. As export sales grow, the company may begin to experience problems supplying the foreign market via exports because of a variety of tariff and nontariff barriers and import restrictions imposed by the local government. Believing that the foreign market should be protected, the company management may resort to licensing a local company to produce the product. This may turn out to be the wrong strategy if in fact the market for the product expands and becomes large enough to support a local production facility. The option of production abroad would be unavailable to the company now because a local company is already producing the product. Had the company looked into the future and made sales forecasts for the product in the foreign market, it might not have given the license to the foreign company to produce the product, and instead could have commenced production itself.

Lack of planning may also "lead to a sub-optimum deployment of corporate resources overseas and a consequent loss of the potential benefits of multinational operations. An important advantage of multinational business as contrasted with purely domestic operations is that it provides management with the broadest possible dimension of enterprise in which to take full advantage of worldwide investment opportunities that offer the highest returns. However, this strength can be realized only when alternatives are systematically examined and compared on a global basis."[8]

Absence of effective planning may result in the company's allocating its resources to ventures that may not represent the best among the available global market opportunities. For instance, a company that does not have a formalized program for the evaluation of foreign market opportunities is not likely to discover the best ones among the many available; therefore it might make an unwise investment abroad merely because the prime opportunities were never identified as such.

Proper timing of entry into foreign markets can often make the difference between success or failure of a foreign venture. Establishing a production facility before the market is large enough to support the required volume for optimum plant utilization results in excess plant capacity and higher per unit production costs. However, waiting too long is always equally undesirable because the first entrant in the market has the distinct advantage of being able to capture a huge share of the total sales volume. And the experience of many companies has shown the difficulty in taking sales and market share away from a competitor who already has a large proportion of the total market. Timing of foreign market entry is thus critical and needs very careful planning.

The availability of adequate resources, both financial and managerial, is often overlooked by firms when they decide to venture abroad. At issue is not the availability of such resources in absolute terms; companies with genuine opportunity can generally manage to find them. What is crucial is that the resources be at hand when they are needed. For instance, a company may be making fine profits, but if its capital is tied up in the development and marketing of many new products that experience a greater cash outflow than cash inflow, it may not have the necessary cash to start new ventures abroad—especially if it does not have a portfolio of mature products which can serve as "cash cows." Or a company could establish many foreign affiliates in rapid succession only to find to its dismay that it does not have adequate managerial personnel to send out from the home office, or hire abroad, to manage these operations. Planning of foreign market entry could avoid such problems.

Finally, lack of planning may cause numerous operating problems after the foreign venture gets under way. For example, a company may assume that marketing channels similar to those at home would be available in the foreign market, only to find that there are no existing channels that it could use for marketing its products. In the United States and other advanced Western countries, a company has the choice between establishing its own distribution network or using one already there—such as a chain of department stores or retail food outlets. Most developing countries do not have such alternative distribution networks, so companies must set up their own, which could be quite expensive. Furthermore, the company may not have anticipated the need to hold a far greater stockpile of inventory of raw materials and components than the level generally kept in the home country. Such stockpiling could be necessary if the items must be imported because they are unavailable locally; this stockpiling will probably mean higher inventory costs than anticipated.

STEPS IN DEVELOPING AN INTERNATIONAL CORPORATE STRATEGY

The aforementioned problems that arise from poor planning point out the acute need for the development of a strategy for international business operations. In the following pages we shall be concerned with how such a strategy may be developed by a company that is considering entering foreign markets, along with some issues involved in the development of the strategy.

A company that is considering foreign market opportunities should begin by asking the following basic questions: Should we go international? If the answer to this question is in the affirmative then the next set of questions to consider are: Where throughout the world should we look for opportunities? How soon should we embark on our first venture abroad? What is the best way of exploiting the foreign opportunities? Although on the surface it may appear that there are many business opportunities abroad, it is important to recognize that such opportunities vary significantly among industries and individual firms. Besides, different firms have unequal abilities to exploit foreign markets successfully. Hence, in evaluating the value of entry into foreign markets management should:

1. Evaluate the opportunities in foreign markets for the firm's products and technology, as well as the potential threats, problems, and risks related to these opportunities.

2. Evaluate the strengths and weaknesses of the firm's managerial, material, technical, and functional (finance, marketing, etc.) competence to determine the degree to which the firm has the resources to successfully exploit potential foreign opportunities.

Step 1 is generally known as *environmental analysis* and step 2 as the *internal resource audit*.

The assessment of the international opportunities, and of the strengths and weaknesses of its resource base should permit the company's management to define the scope of its international business involvement. The next step is to formulate the companywide international business objectives; this is followed by the development of pertinent international corporate strategies aimed at achieving companywide international business objectives.

To summarize, the development of an international corporate strategy involves the following steps:

1. Evaluate the international opportunities, threats, problems, and risks;

2. Evaluate the strengths and weaknesses of the firm to exploit the foreign opportunities;

3. Define the scope of the firm's international business involvement;

4. Formulate the firm's international corporate objectives;

5. Develop specific corporate strategies for the firm as a whole.

It should be noted that although the steps are listed sequentially in the preceding list, in practice the process is iterative, and there is, typically, considerable backtracking as one progresses from one step to the next. For example, if international business objectives are formulated but then managers cannot develop creditable strategies to achieve them, the objectives must be changed and steps 4 and 5 redone. The entire process is illustrated in Figure 3–1. Let us now examine the steps in international corporate strategy formulation.

Analyzing the International Environment

Environmental analysis focuses on discovery and evaluation of business opportunities and on the threats, problems, and risks associated with

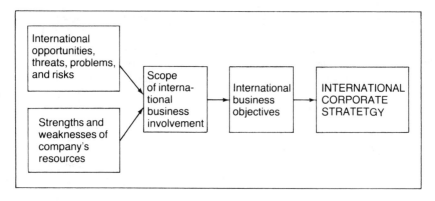

FIGURE 3-1 *International Corporate Strategy Process*

them. It involves the analysis of certain factors in the environment that could have a significant positive or negative impact on the operations of a firm, and over which the firm has little or no control. Environmental factors with a positive impact may create future opportunities whereas those with a negative impact may represent future threats, risks, and problems for the firm. Such factors—which we shall call the critical environmental factors—are the focus of environmental analysis. Hence, when a firm conducts an environmental analysis it should zero in on the critical factors in the economic, political, legal, and cultural segments of the total environment in which the firm operates.

International environmental analysis is the conduct of this activity on an international scale. However, in an international company, environmental analysis should be conducted on at least three different levels: (1) multinational, (2) regional, and (3) country. At the *multinational level*, environmental analysts at the company headquarters are concerned with the identification, forecasting, and monitoring of critical environmental factors in the world at large. The analysis is of a very broad nature, devoid of much detail; its focus is the significant trends and events unfolding over time. For example, corporate environmental analysts may study the global technological developments, or trends in governmental intervention in the economies of nations, or the overall changes occurring in the values and lifestyles of people in industrialized versus developing countries. Then the analysts would make judgments about the probable nature of the these trends and the degree of impact on the internal operations of the company—now and in the future.

Environmental analysis at the *regional level* focuses on a more detailed study of the critical environmental factors within a specific geographic area such as Western Europe, the Middle East, or Southeast Asia. Here the intent is to identify opportunities for marketing the company's products, services, or technology in a particular region. Analysts also research the types of problems that may occur and the appropriate strategies to counter them. For example, an automobile company may find that the significant growth anticipated in the gross national product and per capita incomes of the population has created a potentially large market for automobiles; however, because of the absence of good roads and skilled auto mechanics, the cars sold in the region must be sturdy, with engines of basic design that do not require complicated repair procedures. Similarly, a company making electronic equipment may find that low wages in the Far East or southern Asia provide the opportunity to significantly lower production costs by transferring the labor-intensive operations to those areas. But it may also face problems in dealing with a labor force that has a different cultural background. Regional environmental analysis pinpoints countries in the region that seem to have the most market potential; these become the focus of country environmental analysis—the next level of analysis.

Environmental analysis at the *country level* is concerned with an in-depth analysis of the critical environmental factors—economic, legal, political, cultural—in a small number of countries. In each country, an evaluation is made of the nature of the opportunities available. The kinds of questions the analysts ask include: (1) How big is the country market for our products, services, or technology? (2) How can the market be served—by exports, licensing, contract manufacturing, or local production? (3) Which of these is the best strategy for entering the country market? (4) Can the country serve as a base for exports to other countries, including the company's home market?

Country analysis also identifies the nature of the potential threats, risks, and problems associated with each form of market entry. For instance, serving the local market through exports to it may carry with it the risk of government restraints in the future, such as higher tarrifs or import quotas. However, establishing a local production facility may be also risky because the government may, in the future, insist that the equity of the foreign affiliate be shared with the local population. Thus, country environmental analysis must be oriented to each of the market entry strategies for it to be meaningful for planning purposes. A suggested procedure for conducting this analysis is as follows: First, identify the critical external conditions or factors that must exist for the success of a particular market entry strategy. Next, evaluate the critical environmental factors associated with each market entry strategy. A matrix similar to that shown in Exhibit 3–1 may be used for this purpose. Evaluations of the critical environmental factors (economic, legal, political, cultural) that can affect each form of market entry are made and recorded symbolically in each cell in the matrix. The individual evaluations in each cell may be "averaged" to arrive at a cumulative index of the quality of the critical environmental factors for each market entry strategy, thus permitting a comparison among them. Similar market entry strategy evaluations may be conducted for each country under consideration. Examples of different types of critical environmental factors for each form of market entry strategy are presented in Exhibit 3–2.

Before closing the subject of international environmental analysis, we must stress that the external environment is always changing and hence the critical environmental factors favorable at one time may become unfavorable later, and vice versa. Therefore, global, regional, and country environmental analysis must be done continuously. Moreover, the focus of such analysis must be upon forecasting the characteristics of the critical environmental factors in the future so that the company may have sufficient lead time to make appropriate modifications in its strategies.

Making an Internal Resources Audit

The focus of external environmental analysis is on the environmental conditions that must be present for the successful implementation of a market entry strategy. Now our attention is turned to the internal resources audit, which is concerned with an evaluation of the conditions internal to the company that must exist if the company is to succeed in a specific business in a particular country. The aim of an internal resource audit is to match the company's managerial, technical, material, and financial resources with those required for success in a business.

The internal resource audit is business related rather than environment related. The *key business success factors* (KBSF) may be different from those needed in another business. For example the factors needed to succeed in the baby food business are different from those required for success in the fast food industry.

The internal resource audit is also country related; for example, the total amount of resources that a firm must have at its command inter-

EXHIBIT 3–1 *Market Entry Strategy Evaluation Matrix*

Critical Environmental Factors / Entry Strategy	Economic	Legal	Political	Cultural	Cumulative Strategy Index
Export	A	C	B	B	B
Licensing	B	A	A	E	A−
Contract Manufacturing	C	B	A	E	B
Local production	B	B	C	B	

A ÷ Excellent   D ÷ Poor
B ÷ Good   E ÷ not applicable
C ÷ Fair   F ÷ not acceptable

EXHIBIT 3-2 *Examples of Critical Environmental Factors for Market Entry Strategies*

Export	Contract Manufacturing
Import tariffs	Quality of local contractor
Import quotas	Capital repatriation
Distance from nearest supplier country	*Local Production*
Freight costs	Political stability
	Size of market
Licensing	Market structure
Patent and trademark protection	Currency stability
Quality of licensee	Capital repatriation
Legal limit on royalty rate structure	Local attitude toward foreign ownership

nally to succeed in a business in a country such as Mali may not be required internally to succeed in Japan. A well-developed capital market and banking industry in Japan, for instance, allows a firm to borrow locally for working capital or plant expansion purposes. It does not have to have this money internally. But the absence of such facilities in Mali would force the firm to finance the foreign affiliate's capital requirements from its internal sources, such as retained earnings. Thus, in order to succeed in the business in Mali, a firm must have the capacity to generate the required funds from internal sources.

Along the same lines, a firm in a business that requires effective channels of distribution, such as vending machines or food markets (such as "Seven-Eleven"), for marketing its products must have the resources to develop its own distribution system. In a country that does not have well-developed channels of distribution, it will have to induce independent retail shop owners to carry and promote their products. Such a problem would not occur in an advanced country like Germany, but would in a developing nation such as Sudan.

The preceding examples show that there is a close link between the strengths and weakness of a firm and the environment in which it does business: a firm may have ample resources to do business in one country but may match up very unsatisfactorily with the setting another country provides. Each environment places constraints on the availability of required resources to succeed in the business in that country's market.

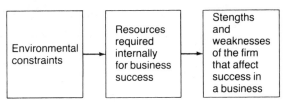

FIGURE 3-2 *Relationship Between External Environmental Constraints and the Strengths and Weaknesses of a Firm*

These constraints determine the amount of resources that the firm must be able to generate on its own in order to succeed. The ability to generate resources determines the firm's strengths and weaknesses. This relationship between the environmental constraints and the firm's strengths and weaknesses is shown in Figure 3–2.

The conceptual process needed to evaluate the strengths and weaknesses of a company is this: (1) Determine the key business success factors, that is, the factors the firm must excel in in order to succeed in the business. (2) Match the firm's available resources against those required to score high and do better than competitors in each of the areas identified by the key business success factors. (3) Assess the strengths and weaknesses of the firm. This process is illustrated in Figure 3–3. Examples of key business success factors are presented in Exhibit 3–3.

The key business success factors can and do change from one time period to another. For example, fuel efficiency was not a critical factor for success in the automobile industry prior to the oil crisis and its resultant increases in the price of gasoline (since 1974); but now it is. Therefore, a company must maintain an effective program for continuously monitoring and forecasting the key factors for success in each of the businesses it is involved in. And an international company must conduct an evaluation of its strengths and weaknesses to succeed in every country in which it already has business operations or is planning to start them in the near future.

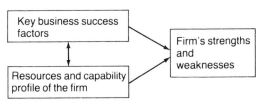

FIGURE 3-3 *Conceptual Process to Evaluate the Strengths and Weaknesses of a Firm*

EXHIBIT 3-3   *Examples of Key Business Success Factors*

Automobile Manufacturer	Pharmaceutical Company
Styling	Efficacy of products
Fuel efficiency	Product innovation
Quality	Patents
Price	Company image
Service	
Distribution system	

Soft Drinks Producer

Channels of distribution
Taste
Sales promotion
Brand identification
Price

Defining the Scope of International Business Involvement

The next step in international corporate strategy formulation is the definition of the scope or basic perimeters of the firm's international business activities. The scope helps the company management identify those foreign market opportunities that may be considered for an in-depth study before resources are committed for their exploitation; those that fall clearly outside the scope can be ignored. A thorough investigation of a foreign market can be costly and time consuming; therefore, defining the company's scope of international business involvement helps the company weed out market opportunities that, given the company's strengths and weaknesses, it cannot exploit.

The scope of the company's international business may be defined in terms of the following dimensions: geography, product, technology, ownership, size of commitment, risk, time span, form of market entry, and level of economic development. The following questions must be answered in each dimension.

• *Geography:* Should the company limit its international business involvement to certain geographic regions of the world, or should it become truly global by going after opportunities that are attractive irrespective of their geographic location?

• *Product:* Should the company's international business involvement be limited to some of its products or to all products? Should the stage in the product life cycle determine a product's international involvement —that is, should only mature products be involved in international business, leaving those that are at the development or growth stage for the home market first?

• *Technology:* Shall the company limit its international activities to those opportunities that involve the use of older or nonproprietary technology? Or should the international thrust be founded on superior and most advanced technology available? How important is patent protection in the transfer of technology abroad?

• *Ownership:* Should the foreign ventures be one hundred percent owned by the company, or can ownership be shared with local partners abroad? Is a majority ownership acceptable in areas where complete ownership is not allowed by local legislation? Under what conditions will a minority ownership be acceptable?

• *Size of Commitment:* Should there be limits placed on the magnitude of commitments the company is willing to consider in a given market? Should maximum and minimum limits be placed on the size of commitments that can be made in one country?

• *Risk:* How much risk is the company willing to assume in a venture, given the size of commitment involved and the benefits expected? What is the balance among risk, commitment, and benefits that is acceptable in each venture? Should risks be diversified by products and regions?

• *Time Span:* What proportion of the company's total resources should be committed to foreign opportunities in any given year? Should the company enter by phases into foreign markets?

• *Form of Market Entry:* Will the company consider only opportunities that are exploitable by local production or will it consider those that lend themselves to exporting, licensing, or other market entry strategies?

• *Level of Economic Development:* Should the company limit its international involvement to developed countries only, or will it consider opportunities in both developed and developing countries?

A deliberate and careful study of these issues will serve to define and limit the scope of the company's international business involvement. For example, one firm may conclude that, given its strengths and weaknesses, it should limit its initial foreign involvement to establishing a firm foothold via licensing in the European Common Market, and it might limit such involvement in the early stages to only one of its major product lines. Another firm may decide to look worldwide for market opportunities, and to exploit them only by establishing wholly owned manufacturing facilities. Thus, defining the scope of international business involvement specifies the types of foreign business opportunities the firm is interested in, allowing it to ignore those that do not meet the chosen criteria.

Formulating International Corporate Objectives

The next step in the international corporate strategy formulation is the determination of what the company hopes to achieve from its international operations. International corporate objectives are the objectives of the company as a whole. They serve as the umbrella under which the objectives of each of its corporate divisions and foreign affiliates are formulated. Divisional and affiliate objectives are expected to be consistent with, and contributory to, the international corporate objectives. This relationship between international corporate, divisional, and affiliate objectives is presented in Figure 3–4.

International corporate objectives are formulated in areas such as profitability, marketing, production, finance, technology, host government relations, personnel, research and development, and the environment. There may be other areas in which international corporate objectives may be formulated. The general guideline is to formulate objectives in areas that directly and vitally affect the survival and prosperity of the company. While developing corporate objectives, top management must recognize the objectives of the so-called claimants on the corporation—the stockholders, customers, employees, suppliers, and the public located in geographically dispersed regions. But most impor-

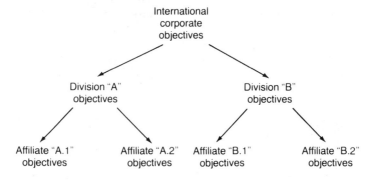

FIGURE 3–4 *The Hierarchy of Objectives*

tantly, top management must make every effort to ensure that the company's foreign operations make positive contributions toward meeting the goals of each host country.

Often the objectives of these various groups conflict with each other, in which case top management must establish their relative importance to the long-run survival and growth of the company; also, management must assess the comparative political influence of each claimant, then reformulate the international corporate objectives in the company's long-range interests. "The importance of recognizing the objectives of the various claimants is brought into sharp focus when we realize that several American multinational companies could have avoided expropriation of their properties in Latin America had they recognized the values . . . and expectations of the host countries and incorporated them in their . . . overall company objectives and plans."[9]

The different areas in which a company may formulate (and revise) its international corporate objectives are presented in Exhibit 3–4.

The next critical task for top management is deciding how the objectives are to be achieved. This involves the formulation of the company's corporate strategies.

EXHIBIT 3–4 *Areas for Formulation of International Corporate Objectives*

Profitability

Level of profits
Return on assets, investment, equity, sales
Yearly profit growth
Yearly earnings per share growth

Marketing

Total sales volume
Market share—worldwide, region, country
Growth in sales volume
Growth in market share
Integration of country markets for marketing efficiency and effectiveness

Production

Ratio of foreign to domestic production volume
Economics of scale via international production integration
Quality and cost control
Introduction of cost efficient production methods

(cont.)

EXHIBIT 3-4   *Cont.*

Finance

Financing of foreign affiliates—retained earnings or local borrowing
Taxation—minimizing tax burden globally
Optimum capital structure
Foreign exchange management—minimizing losses from foreign fluctuations

Technology

Type of technology to be transferred abroad—new or old generation
Adaptation of technology to local needs and circumstances

Host Government Relations

Adapting affiliate plans to host government developmental plans
Adherence to local laws, customs, and ethical standards

Personnel

Development of managers with global orientation
Management development of host country nationals

Research and Development

Innovation of patentable products
Innovation of patentable production technology
Geographical dispersion of research and development laboratories

Environment

Harmony with the physical and biological environment
Adherence to local environmental legislation

Developing Specific Corporate Strategies

A strategy may be defined as a course of action designed to achieve a desired end result. Corporate strategy development is concerned with the deployment of the company's resources in order to achieve its international corporate objectives. Corporate strategies, therefore, should be developed in each area in which corporate objectives have been developed.

A corporate strategy establishes the framework for the formulation of strategies at the divisional and foreign affiliate level. For example, a corporate financial strategy that states that all company growth objectives will be financed only by retained earnings implies a very conservative way of financing growth. However, all foreign affiliates must abide by this companywide strategy and finance their own growth plans only by retained earnings. Similarly, a corporate marketing strategy calling for the adaptation of products to suit the local tastes and conditions allows the foreign affiliates to make the appropriate changes in the basic product, but it forbids the introduction of new products. For example, a company involved in the marketing of coffee worldwide may allow the local affiliates to modify its taste to suit local preferences, but it will not allow an affiliate to sell a product such as cocoa, which may be new to the company.

Corporate strategies affect the fundamental design of a company's overall operations. An analogy with the design of an aircraft may help to explain this concept. An aerospace engineer who changes the design of an airplane to achieve its performance objectives is involved in "corporate strategy" formulation, and the design of all components of the airplane must conform with the overall airplane design. Similarly the design of the company's overall operations constrains and influences the design of the divisional and affiliate operations.

Although corporate strategies are formulated in the areas that are of major concern to the company, which will therefore vary from one company to another, international companies do develop strategies in some areas common to all; consider the following:

- Methods of entering foreign markets
- Growth—internal development versus acquisitions
- Geographical diversification
- Product diversification
- Product portfolio optimization
- Foreign exchange risk management
- Human resources development
- Organization structure.

The construction of corporate strategy is a difficult process. It requires an objective assessment of the strengths and weaknesses of the company's resources and of its managerial practices. Adoption of new strategies may mean the abandoning of old and familiar ways of running a business and therefore may, as a prerequisite, involve a change in the fundamental attitudes of top management. However difficult the process may be, top management must evaluate corporate strategies periodically and keep them in tune with the dynamic environment.

To repeat a point that was made earlier in this chapter, the entire corporate strategy formulation process is by nature iterative. The essence of the entire process is to keep the organization adaptable and responsive to changes. Hence, every step in the corporate strategy formulation process we have discussed must be performed in view of the present and forecasted characteristics of the firm's environment.

SUMMARY

This chapter was about the process of planning in an international company, from the point of view of the top management personnel at the headquarters of an international company.

Planning is one of the basic functions of management. It is a process that involves the assessment of the environment for opportunities and threats, the evaluation of the strengths and weaknesses of the enterprise, and the formulation of objectives and strategies designed to exploit the future opportunities and combat the threats.

International planning is planning in an international context. Planning in an international company is far more complicated than in a domestic company because the multinational environment in which an international company's operations and activities occur is far more complex than that of its purely domestic counterpart.

International companies have to confront several significant external and internal issues and problems in global planning, such as: political instability and risk, currency instability, competition from state-owned enterprises, pressures from national governments, nationalism, patent and trademark protection, and intense competition. Examples of internal problems and issues are: integrating the foreign and domestic units, centralized control versus decentralized initiative, developing managers with an international perspective, internalizing environmental information, and worldwide resource allocation.

After discussing briefly the nature of problems created when a firm enters foreign markets without proper planning, the chapter was concluded with a coverage of the steps involved in the development of an international corporate strategy.

QUESTIONS

1. Discuss some of the issues and problems that international companies must confront in planning their global operations. Are any of these faced by companies that do not operate internationally?

2. Why is the formulation of an overall plan and a well-designed strategy for entry into foreign markets so critical for an international company?

3. Discuss the three levels at which environmental analysis must take place in an international company. Why should country environmental analysis be oriented to each market entry strategy?

4. "The internal resource audit is both business and country related"—discuss this statement with examples.

FURTHER READING

1. Ackoff, Russel A. *A Concept of Corporate Planning.* New York: Wiley–Interscience, 1970.

2. LaPalombara, Joseph, and Blank, Stephen. *Multinational Corporations in Comparative Perspective.* New York: The Conference Board, 1977.

3. Phatak, Arvind V. *Managing Multinational Corporations.* New York: Praeger Publishers, 1974.

4. Schwendiman, John S. *Strategic and Long-Range Planning for the Multinational Corporation.* New York: Praeger Publishers, 1973.

5. Steiner, George A. *Top Management Planning.* New York: Macmillan, 1969.

6. Walters, Kenneth D., and Monsen, R. José. "State-owned Business Abroad: New Competitive Threat." *Harvard Business Review,* March–April 1979.

7. Yoshino, M. Y. "International Business: What Is the Best Strategy?" *The Business Quarterly,* Fall 1966.

NOTES

1. Russell A. Ackoff, *A Concept of Corporate Planning* (New York: Wiley–Interscience, 1970), p. 1.
2. Ibid., p. 4.
3. George A. Steiner, *Top Management Planning* (New York: Macmillan, 1969), p. 6.
4. Ibid.
5. See Kenneth D. Walters and R. Joseph Monsen, "State-Owned Business Abroad: New Competitive Threat," *Harvard Business Review,* March–April 1979, pp. 160 –70.
6. John Snow Schwendiman, *Strategic and Long-Range Planning for the Multinational Corporation* (New York: Praeger Publishers, 1973), p. 87.

3. PLANNING IN AN INTERNATIONAL SETTING

7. Joseph LaPalombara and Stephen Blank, *Multinational Corporations in Comparative Perspective* (New York: The Conference Board, 1977), p. xiv.
8. M. Y. Yoshino, "International Business: What is the Best Strategy," *The Business Quarterly*, Fall 1966, p. 47.
9. Arvind V. Phatak, *Managing Multinational Corporations* (New York: Praeger Publishers, 1974), p. 162.

Chapter **4**

Organizing
for International Operations

Organizations are "created to link the behavior of individuals: to collect and pool information, skills, or capital; to engage in related actions toward the achievement of a set of goals; to monitor performance, initiate corrections, and define new goals."[1] In a strictly domestic enterprise, these aims can be achieved with a two-dimensional organization—an organization that concerns itself with resolving the potentially conflicting demands of functional (production, finance, marketing, etc.) and product-line requirements. A two-dimensional organization is, however, not the appropriate structure for a multinational enterprise because it must be able to resolve functional and product-line demands, but also to deal effectively with geographic area concerns. Thus, a more appropriate organizational form for a multinational enterprise should combine three dimensions: (1) functional expertise, (2) product and technical know-how, and (3) knowledge of the area and country. The manner in which these three dimensions are combined should and does differ from one international company to another. There is no one best way for organizing an international company, and each company will combine these three dimensions in an organizational structure that it tries to make consistent with its particular strategy.

Michael Duerr and John Roach point out that a firm's international organization is generally determined as a response to three major strategic concerns:

- How to encourage a predominantly domestic organization to take full advantage of growth opportunities abroad.
- How to blend product knowledge and geographic area knowledge most efficiently in coordinating worldwide business.
- How to coordinate the activities of foreign units in many countries while permitting each to retain its own identity.[2]

Responses to each of these concerns will differ, depending on the firm's situation and the overall philosophy of top management.

In this chapter we shall be focusing on the organizational design of international enterprises, that is, on the formal arrangement of relationships between the various domestic and foreign organizational units in the multinational network and the mechanisms provided for their coordination into a unified whole. The treatment will be limited to the level of the senior managers who report directly to the president's office. We shall not be concerned with the organizational structure of foreign affiliates; rather the emphasis will be on the structure inside the parent company, whose purpose is to plan and control the multinational network, and on the structure of the network itself. The treatment of organization structure excludes recognition of the legal or statutory features of an enterprise. The legal structure is classified, in accordance with government regulations, for tax and cash-flow purposes. It seldom reflects the actual manner in which an enterprise is managed. Because this chapter is concerned with managerial aspects of an international company, the legal structure has been ignored.

Six basic organizational structures of multinational companies will be covered: the preinternational division phase; and the structures of the international division, the global product, the global area, the global function, and the multidimensional global form.

BASIC ORGANIZATIONAL DESIGN OF INTERNATIONAL ENTERPRISES

In most cases, a multinational firm's organizational structure is neither predetermined nor permanently fixed, but rather is seen as one that evolves continuously to correspond with changes in the firm's strategy. As a firm's operations grow and spread to new foreign markets, its organizational structure typically becomes overburdened. As the strain intensifies and threatens organizational structure, the firm is normally compelled to experiment with alternate organizational forms; eventually it chooses one consistent with its new international expansionist strategy and capable of handling its expanding operations. The replacement structure chosen is typically influenced by the structure that preceded it because the experience of the company with one structure provides the building blocks for future structures.

Although there is no one best organizational structure for multinational enterprises, it does not follow that every firm's organizational structure is completely unique or that there is no rationale to a firm's structural development. On the contrary, there are certain regular organizational patterns that firms of like strategy develop and through which multinational firms with changing strategies evolve.

PREINTERNATIONAL DIVISION PHASE

The early patterns of development of international firms appear to parallel the stages of development of the so-called product cycle. According to this cycle (see Figure 4–1), a firm with a technologically advanced product in the new-product stage is well positioned to exploit foreign markets. Generally, initial exploitation occurs through exports—the first stage in the evolution of a multinational company. At this stage, the firm is relatively small by multinational enterprise standards, and its activities are generally confined to a few products and markets. (Different stages in the evolution of a multinational enterprise were covered in Chapter 1.)

The firm has to deal with a comparatively limited number of

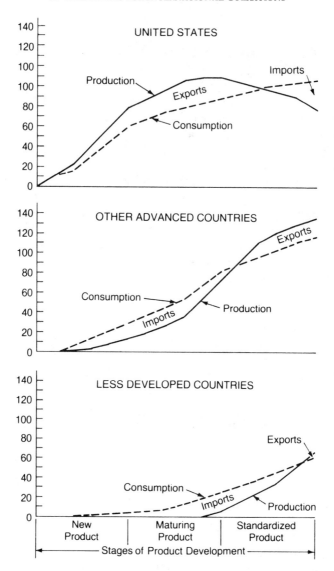

FIGURE 4-1 *International Trade and Production in the Product Cycle*
SOURCE: *Raymond Vernon and Louis T. Wells, Jr.*, Manager in the International Economy, *4th edition (Englewood Cliffs, N.J.: Prentice-Hall, Inc, 1981), p. 94.*

strategic dimensions, most of which are related to the domestic market, and which can be addressed directly by the president with input from managers who report directly to him. Since the firm's technologically advanced product stands on its own, there is little need to develop expertise in the foreign markets in which the firm sells. Assistance in exporting is usually provided initially by an independent export management company and later by an inhouse export manager. In most cases, an inhouse export manager is thought of as an adjunct to marketing, whose principal communication needs are with the marketing vice-president and others in the marketing group. The organizational arrangements for a firm in this stage of multinational development are rather simple, with an export manager reporting to the chief marketing officer in an organization with a narrow product line; or directly to the chief executive officer in an organization with a broad product line (see Figure 4–2).

As the firm's exports increase and its product matures, certain

A. Company with narrow product line

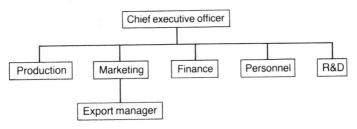

B. Company with broad product line

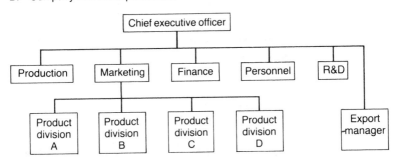

FIGURE 4–2 *Typical Organization of International Company Primarily Engaged in Exporting to Foreign Markets.*

FIGURE 4-3 *Typical Organization of Company at Early Foreign Production Stage*

pressures develop that tend to threaten the firm's foreign market share. Such threats originate from two sources: (1) Others at home and abroad begin to share the firm's special knowledge and special skills. Thus the threat of competition becomes more tangible. (2) As local demand and sales volume increase in a country, an importing country begins to encourage local production by imposing "buy-local" policies on its government agencies and other public buyers and by enacting import restrictions such as tariffs and quotas.

Faced with increased competition from other producers and higher comparative costs resulting from freight and tariff costs, the exporting firm feels pressed to defend its foreign market position by establishing a production facility inside the foreign market. Once established, the foreign production unit supplies the foreign market as the former technologically advanced product matures or makes its way through the maturity stage and into the standardized product stage of the product cycle. The same cycle may be repeated by the firm in the markets of other nations as the firm tries to protect its market share by establishing local production units to supply the local markets. At the first the management of the newly formed foreign subsidiaries remains quite decentralized. A typical organizational arrangement for a firm at this early stage of foreign production is shown in Figure 4-3. Here the foreign subsidiaries report directly to the company president or other designated company officer who carries out his responsibilities without assistance from a headquarters staff group. As the firm increases its investment in foreign operating units, however, and as these become more important to the firm's overall performance, greater emphasis is placed on international product coordination and operations control.

Thus, there is pressure to assemble a headquarters staff group to assist the officer in charge and to develop a specialized international expertise. While originally responsible for the firm's foreign operating units, the group essentially takes control of all international activities of the firm and evolves into a separate international division in a new and comparatively more complex organizational structure.

THE INTERNATIONAL DIVISION STRUCTURE

In the international division form of organization, all international activities are grouped into one separate division and assigned to a senior executive at the corporate headquarters. The senior executive is often given the title of vice-president of the international division or director of international operations, and is at the same level as the other divisional and functional heads of the company in the organizational hierarchy (see Figure 4–4).

The head of the international division is generally given line authority over the subsidiaries abroad, and the international division is made into a profit center. The formation of the international division in effect segregates the company's overall operations into two differentiated parts—domestic and international. As far as the top management at the headquarters is concerned, the international division is expected to manage the nondomestic operations and therefore to be the locus of whatever international expertise there is or should be in the company. There is not much contact or integration between the domestic and international side, and whatever coordination there is between the two

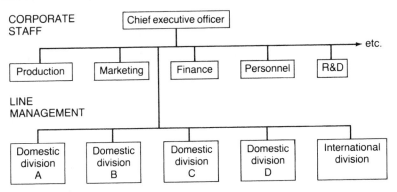

FIGURE 4-4 *International Division Structure*

segments of the company occurs at the company's top management level.

Organizationally, the formation of an international division lessens the autonomy of the foreign subsidiaries because authority to make strategic decisions is pulled up into the hands of the head of the international division. However, this change is also accompanied by a far greater measure of guidance and support from the top to the foreign subsidiaries.

Who Adopts the International Division Structure

In general, the companies that are still at the developmental stages of international business involvement are likely to adopt the international division structure. Other factors favoring the adoption of this structure are: limited product diversity; comparatively small sales (compared to domestic and export sales) generated by foreign subsidiaries; limited geographic diversity; and few executives with international expertise.

In the international division, the executives are able to supervise the establishment and growth of one or more product lines in several foreign markets and at the same time develop new opportunities for expansion in others; in this structure, the executives are providing the concentration of managerial expertise necessary for the effective promotion of the company's international efforts. During the period the company is establishing itself in the international markets, international operations tend to remain, in the minds of the other corporate executives of domestic operations, a sideline of minor importance.

There are several advantages to the use of an international division structure. The concentration of international executives within the division ensures that the special needs of emerging foreign operations are met. The presence of the head of the international operations as a member of the top management planning team serves as a constant reminder to top management of the global implications of all decisions. The international group provides a unified position to the company's activities in different countries and regions as efforts are made to coordinate the operations of foreign subsidiaries with respect to the various functional areas—finance, marketing, purchasing, and production. For example, central coordination of international activities "enables the company to make more secure and more economic decisions about where to purchase raw materials, where to locate new manufacture, and from where to supply world customers with products. Also, when the financial function of the international division is coordinated, investment decisions can be made on a global basis and overseas development can turn to international capital markets, instead of just local ones, for funds."[3] The international division also does not strain the capabilities of product or functional managers within the domestic divisions because these persons are not required to work with unfamiliar environments.

There are several drawbacks to the international division structure; hence a company will use this structure only if the benefits from its adoption as a coordinating mechanism clearly outweigh the costs. The principal disadvantages of the international division structure are the following: The separation and isolation of domestic managers from their international counterparts may prove to be a severe handicap as the company continues to expand abroad. If the foreign operations should approach a level of equality with the domestic ones in terms of size, sales, and profits the ability of the domestic managers to think and act strategically on a global scale could be critical to the success of the company. An independent international division may also put constraints on top management's efforts to mobilize and allocate resources of the company globally to achieve overall corporate objectives. "Even with superb coordination at the corporate level, global planning for individual products or product lines is carried out at best awkwardly by two 'semi-autonomous' organizations—the domestic company and the international division."[4] Conflicts occasionally occur between the domestic product divisions and the international division, particularly when the international division asks for help from the domestic divisions and gets what it considers to be inadequate technical support and second-rate staff members for special assignments abroad. Still another problem with the international division is that the firm's research and development remains domestically oriented. Consequently new ideas originating abroad for new products or processes are not easily transmitted and enthusiastically tackled by the research and development personnel, who remain, after all, in the domestic setting of the organization.

When Is an International Division No Longer Appropriate?

As international sales and production capacity grow, and as more markets are entered, product lines begin to diversify to serve a variety of end users. Then considerations such as transfer pricing (charging a higher or lower price between divisions than is charged to an outside buyer) come into play; the international division structure gets strained to its limits and is unable to fulfill its former role. Faced with this situation, the company may continue to use the international division structure by further subdivision as a response to diversification—either by product line, if product diversification is causing the problem, or by geography, if regional diversification is straining the organization (see Figure 4-5). Product or area managers, reporting to the international division head, are then established within the division to coordinate the expansion of the firm into new markets.

Another alternative is to take the profit responsibility from the international division and reorganize the entire company on either a product or area division basis, keeping the international division in an advisory capacity. (The product- and area-based structures will be discussed later in the chapter.) If given an advisory role, executives in the division can function as generalists—monitoring environmental trends and conditions and advising their functional, product, or geographical counterparts in the company. If the firm chooses to reorganize on a product basis, the international staff might be assigned to monitor the legal, political, cultural, and economic environments of major country and

A. By area

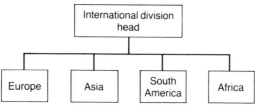

B. By product

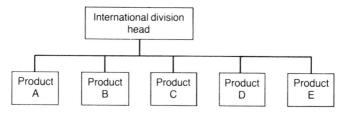

FIGURE 4-5   *Divisonalization Within the International Division*

regional markets. If a geographically based structure is chosen, the international staff may serve as global coordinators, spotting trends and continuing to investigate the potential for new markets.

A *Business International* research report identifies the following factors as indicators that the international division is no longer an appropriate structure for an international company:

- The international market is as important as the domestic market
- Senior officials of the corporation have both foreign and domestic experience
- International sales represent 25 to 35 percent of total sales
- The technology used in domestic divisions has far outstripped that of the international division.[5]

Other studies have shown that the pressures to reorganize on an integrated worldwide basis by dismantling the international division mount when it has grown large enough to be equal to the size of the largest product division.[6] This is to a large extent because of the struggles that take place between the international and domestic divisions over capital budgeting and transfer pricing issues.[7] But most importantly, it is the structural conflict between the geographic orientation of the international division and the product orientation of the domestic divisions that motivates top management to reorganize the company in a fashion that merges the domestic and international sides of the business into one integrated global structure.

GLOBAL STRUCTURES

Up to this point we have been concentrating on the typical stages in the evolution of the organizational structure of a company as it becomes increasingly involved in international business activities. As the firm gains experience in operating internationally, and as the initial limited involvement in foreign direct investment gradually turns into a full-fledged commitment by top management to perceive the company as a truly multinational enterprise, the company enters a new phase in its evolution: the domestic–foreign bifurcation is abandoned in favor of an integrated worldwide orientation.

Strategic decisions that previously were made separately for the domestic and international parts of the company are henceforth made at the corporate headquarters for the total enterprise, without any distinctions of domestic versus foreign. Top management considers the home market to be only one of many, and the operational and staff groups are given global responsibility. Under such an attitudinal setup at the corporate headquarters, corporate decisions are made with a total company perspective and for the purpose of achieving the company's overall mission and objectives. These decisions include where to establish a new production facility, where to raise capital, what businesses and products to be in, where to obtain the resources, the methods to be used for tapping foreign markets, subsidiary ownership policies, and so on.

The shift to a global orientation in company management must be accompanied by the acquisition and allocation of company resources on the basis of global opportunities and threats; these changes require an organizational structure that is consistent with and supportive of this new managerial posture. The new organizational structure includes, as all structures do to varying degrees, three types of informational inputs: product, geography, and function. Although the structures adopted by various companies differ, the structure an international company adopts is certain to be based on one of these basic orientations: a worldwide area or a worldwide product (or occasionally, a worldwide function). "Depending on which is chosen, delineation of the other dimension[s] . . . are accounted for, in sequence. For these secondary and tertiary forces, they are subdivided (and hence duplicated) with each primary grouping, and/or they are centrally positioned in the form of corporate staff."[8]

We shall begin the study of global structures by first examining the product structure.

The Global Product Division

When the international division is discarded in favor of a global product division, the domestic divisions are given worldwide responsibility for product groups. The manager in charge of a product division is given the line authority and responsibility for the worldwide management of all functional activities—such as finance, marketing, production, etc.—related to a product or product group. Within each product division, there may exist an international unit or even a more refined subdivisionalization on an area basis (see Figure 4-6).

Each product division functions as a semiautonomous profit center. Divisional management has considerable decentralized authority to run the division because of the unique multinational environmental pres-

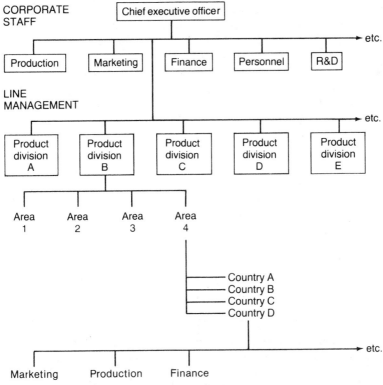

FIGURE 4-6 *Global Product Division Structure*

sures that it must operate under. However corporate headquarters provides the umbrella of the companywide plans and corporate strategy. This umbrella provides both the protection and the constraints under which product divisions are expected to formulate divisional plans and strategy. A product division receives general functional support from staff groups at the corporate level, but it may also have at the divisional level its own functional staff, specialized to provide services tailored to the division's unique market situation. The product division head is given a worldwide responsibility to develop and promote his product line.

When Is a Global Product Division the Best Choice?

Conditions favoring this structure are these: the firm manufactures products that require different technologies and that have dissimilar end users; foreign sales entail high shipping costs, tariffs, and other restrictions that dictate local manufacturing; there can be little use of common marketing tools and channels of distribution among the firm's products; there exists a significant need to integrate production, marketing, and research related to the product; abroad, there is little need for local product knowledge and product adaptation; or the products involved need continuous technical service and inputs, and a high level of technological capability, requiring, therefore, a close coordination between divisional staff groups and production centers abroad.

Firms whose products have reached the maturity stage in their respective product life cycles in the home market but which are at the earlier growth stage in the foreign market require close product-oriented technological and marketing coordination between the home market affiliates and foreign affiliates. This interdependence between the home and foreign affiliates—the latter needing help from the former in matters pertaining to the production and promotion of the growth product in the foreign market—calls for products, and not markets, as the primary organizing dimension.[9]

In order to maximize the benefits of divisionalization based on the global product structure, a firm must be able to produce a standardized product that requires very minor modifications for individual markets and for which world markets can be developed. Division managers are expected to take advantage of the structure to generate global economies of scale in production, resource acquisition, and market supply. This makes the structure particularly suited to firms that use capital-intensive technology.

The major advantages of this form of organization are the ease and directness of flow of technology and product knowledge from the divisional level to the foreign subsidiaries and back—which tends to put all facilities, regardless of location, on a comparable technological level. Other advantages of this structure are these: it preserves product emphasis and promotes product planning on a global basis; it provides a direct line of communications from the customer to those in the organization who have product knowledge and expertise, thus enabling research and development to work on development of products that serve the needs of the world customer; and it permits line and staff managers within the division to gain an expertise in the technical and marketing aspects of products assigned to them.[10]

In addition, the global product-division structure facilitates the coordination of the domestic and foreign production facilities according to natural resource availability, local labor cost and skill level, tariff and tax regulations, shipping costs, and even climate—in order to produce the highest quality product possible at the lowest cost.

What Are the Drawbacks of a Global Product Division?

There are several critical problems associated with the global product structure. One is the duplication of facilities and staff groups that takes place as each division develops its own infrastructure to support its operations in various regions and countries of the world. Another is that division managers may pursue geographic areas that offer immediate growth prospects for their products and neglect other areas where the current prospects might not be as bright but which may have a far greater long-run potential. A far more serious problem is that of "motivating product division managers to pursue the international market when the preponderance of their current profits comes from domestic business and most of their experience has been domestic."[11]

International companies have tried to alleviate these difficulties by adopting a multidimensional structure, which we will discuss later in this chapter.

The Global Area Division

Firms abandoning the international division may choose to coordinate their global operations by using area (or geography) as the dominant organizational dimension.

In the international division structure, the company's worldwide operations are grouped into two regions—domestic and international. Thus, in a way, the international division structure is also an area-based structure. But in a truly area-based global structure, the company's worldwide operations are grouped into several coequal geographical areas, and the head of an area division is given the line authority and responsibility over all affiliates in the area. There is no one fixed pattern for carving up the geographical areas. Obviously, each enterprise has its own circumstances and needs that determine how countries get grouped into regions. Factors such as location of affiliates, customers, and sources of raw materials influence the grouping of countries into manageable geographic units.

The Domestic Market as One of Many

The area structure reflects a very significant change in the attitudes of top management towards international operations and how the com-

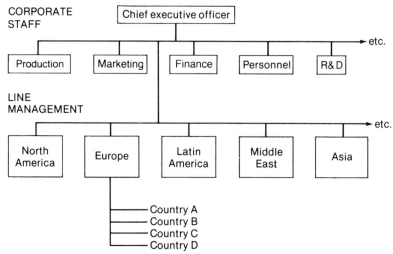

FIGURE 4-7 *Global Area Division Structure*

pany's resources should be allocated. In the international division structure, the domestic and nondomestic bifurcation of the company's global operations reflect a point of view of top management that the domestic side of the business was as important as all the international operations together; but the area structure embodies the attitude that the domestic market is just one of the many markets in the world (see Figure 4-7).

The manager in charge of an area is responsible for the development of business in his region. However, his area plans and strategies have to be consistent with those of the company as a whole. The area manager and his counterparts participate in the formulation of companywide plans and strategies. Such participation in total company planning gives each area manager an appreciation of how his area operations and results fit with the total company plans and performance.

Products Are at the Maturity Stage

Companies using the product division structure have products in the foreign markets which are at the growth stage in the product lifecycle, whereas companies using the area-based structure have products in world markets that have already passed the growth stage and are now at the maturity stage. The products serve common end-user markets and are no longer unique; competitive edge is no longer available from the possession of a distinctive technology. Hence, companies emphasize marketing rather than technology in their competitive strategies, with price and product differentiation being the dominant weapon for retaining market share and sales volume.

When Is a Global Division the Best Choice?

The global area structure is most suited to companies having these characteristics: they are mature businesses with narrow product lines; they have high levels of regional product differentiation, which must obtain high levels of economies of scale from production, marketing, and resource purchase integration on a regional basis; and they feel the need to lower manufacturing costs by utilizing large production runs in large plants using stable technology. Industries with these characteristics which favor the area structure include pharmaceuticals, cosmetics, food, beverage, automotive, and container companies.

The principal advantage of the area structure is that authority to make decisions is pushed down to the regional headquarters. This means that decisions on matters such as product adaptation, price, channels of distribution, and promotion can be made near the scene of action. Information on differences among regions and country markets can be considered at lower levels in the organizational hierarchy, which helps in the making of plans and strategies consistent with the existing regional and country conditions. The other advantage of this structure is that it promotes the finding of regional solutions to problems. Ideas and techniques that have worked in one country are easier to transfer to other countries in the region. And the area manager can resolve conflicts between subsidiaries by finding solutions that optimize the operations in the region as a whole. For example, when a new country market opens up, which subsidiary in the region is in the best position to serve it through exports? Conflicts could occur if more than one subsidiary attempts to export to the new market, but with the area structure, the area manager is in a position to resolve such problems.

What Are the Drawbacks of a Global Area Division?

The main disadvantage of the area structure is the difficulty encountered in reconciling product emphasis with a geographically oriented management approach. This can be particularly difficult if the company's product line is diverse and if it has to be marketed through different types of distribution channels. Since a certain amount of product expertise has to be developed by the area unit, a duplication of product development and technical knowledge is often required. At the same time there is an overlap of functional staff responsibilities with the worldwide headquarters. All of this adds to overhead costs and creates an additional tier of communications.

Other difficulties reported by executives in a study by the Conference Board are that "research and development programs are hard to coordinate, that global product-planning is difficult, that there is no consistent effort to apply newly developed domestic products to international markets, and that introduction to the domestic market of products developed overseas is too slow—or simply that 'product knowledge is weak.'"[12]

In many respects, the advantages of the global area structure are the disadvantages of the global product division structure, and vice versa. The answer to the product/area dilemma may be in an organization structure that incorporates in its authority and responsibility and communications lines a blend of these two dimensions.

The Global Functional Division

The functional dimension is not commonly used by international companies; however, one important exception is the extractive industry—companies that extract oil or metals, for example.

In this form of organization, global operations are organized primarily on a functional basis and secondarily on area or product basis, with marketing and production being the dominant functions. The functional structure is most appropriate for firms with narrow, standardized product lines for which product knowledge is the significant factor (see Figure 4-8).

The main advantages of this form of organization are these: there is an emphasis on functional acumen; it provides tight centralized controls, requiring a relatively lean managerial staff; and it ensures that the power and prestige of the basic activities of the enterprise will be defended by the top managers. The disadvantages of the structure are the following: coordination of manufacturing and marketing in an area (for example, Europe) is problematic; multiple product lines can become difficult to manage because of the separation of production and marketing into departments with parallel lines of authority to the top of the hierarchy; and only the chief executive officer can be held accountable for the profits.

A variant of the global functional structure is the functional process structure used by the petroleum industry. In it, specialized func-

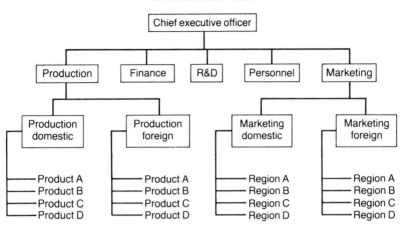

FIGURE 4-8 *Global Functional Structure*

tions—such as exploration, crude production, tanker and pipeline transportation, refining (manufacturing), and marketing—are organized and managed on a global basis through centralized functional departments. These global functional departments may in turn be divisionalized on a geographic area basis (see Figure 4–9). Companies that favor the global functional process-structure are those that: (1) need a tight centralized coordination and control of an integrated production process consisting of stages that are performed on a global basis; and (2) are involved in a major way in transporting products and raw materials across national boundaries, and from one geographic area of the world to another.

The global functional structure has proved to be quite unstable; most companies that adopt it eventually have to abandon it, owing to the problems of integration of supply and distribution caused by the global

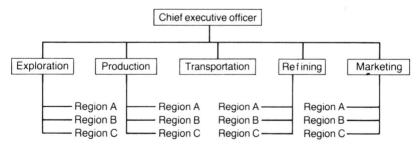

FIGURE 4-9 *Global Functional Process Structure*

dichotomy between production and sales. Commenting on the instability of this form of organization structure, Stanley M. Davis says: "The lesson is, don't organize global structures around functions unless you are in extractive raw materials industries, and even then you will find that they are unstable and will have to share primacy with geographic factors and, in some instances, with product differences."[13]

THE MULTIDIMENSIONAL GLOBAL STRUCTURE

In deciding whether to organize on a functional, product, or area basis, managers of international companies must weigh the benefits of each against the costs. The particular dimension that is chosen as the primary basis for organizing the company's operations is that which offers the best benefits/costs ratio. When one of these three dimensions—function, product, area—is chosen as the primary organizational form, management still tries to utilize the advantages of the remaining two dimensions at lower levels in the structure. For example, a company that is organized on a product division basis may have its own functional staff at the divisional level, and each of the divisions may be further subdivided on a geographic basis. However, many international companies have found that none of the global structures discussed earlier is a totally satisfactory means of organizing because some problems remain untouchable, therefore unsolved. For instance, the problem of coordinating subsidiaries in different divisions on a regional basis in a global product division structure still remains. Similarly, in an organization based on global area, problems still occur in coordinating products on a global basis and across area division lines.

Some companies have attempted to cope with these problems by establishing product committees in area-based structures and area committees in product-based structures. Membership of such committees is comprised of divisional managers and staff specialists who are assigned the collective responsibility for coordinating transactions that cut across divisional lines.

Another alternative is to create staff positions for advisors and counselors. For instance, a product division structure might have area specialists for each of the major regions served by the company; these persons are given the task of exploring new opportunities and developing new markets for the company's products in their respective regions, thus maintaining the distinct advantages of the product structure without losing sight of the unique characteristics of each regional market. Similarly, in an area-based structure, the position of product manager would have responsibility for the coordination of the production and development of his or her product line across geographic areas.

In each of the preceding structural arrangements, there is an implicit assumption that an organizational structure can have only one dominant dimension. Because the advantages of the other dimensions are lost when only one is chosen, an attempt is sometimes made to correct the situation by overlaying the dominant dimension with some aspects of the others.

Some international companies are rejecting the notion that there must be a clear line of authority flowing from the top to the bottom in the organizational hierarchy—with a manager at a given level reporting to only one superior at the next higher level in the hierarchy. This so-called principle of the unity of command has been cast aside by companies that have adopted what is known as the *matrix structure*. In the matrix, the organization avoids choosing one dimension over another as the basis for grouping its operations; instead it chooses two or more: "the foreign subsidiaries report simultaneously to more than one divisional headquarters; worldwide product divisions share with area divisions responsibility for the profits of the foreign subsidiaries."[14]

For instance, a subsidiary manager may report to an area manager as well as a product manager. In a pure product division or area structure, only the manager in charge of the dominant dimension has line authority over a foreign subsidiary in her or his unit; in a matrix structure, both product and area managers have some measure of line authority over the subsidiary. Thus the unity of command principle is abrogated in favor of a coordinating mechanism that considers differences in products and areas to be of equal importance. Firms using the matrix structure are attempting to integrate their operations across more than one dimension simultaneously (Figure 4–10).

Firms should consider adopting the matrix structure if conditions such as the following exist.

- Substantial product and area diversification
- Need to be responsive simultaneously to product and area demands
- Constraints on resources requiring that they be shared by two or more divisions—product, area, or functional

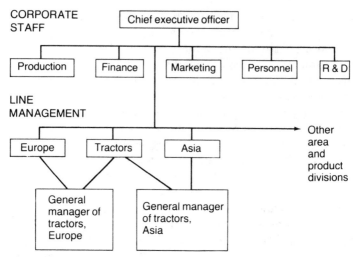

FIGURE 4-10   *The Matrix Structure*

- Significant problems created and opportunities lost due to emphasis on just one dimension, product, or area
- Formulation of corporate strategy requiring the simultaneous consideration of functional, product, and area concerns.

Adoption of a matrix structure requires a commitment on the part of top management, not only to the structure itself but to the essential preparation required for it to be successful. Executive groundwork must be laid; executives must understand how the system works and those— such as the subsidiary managers—who report to two or more superior managers must be prepared to work through the initial confusion created by dual reporting relationships. As noted by Davis and Lawrence, a "matrix organization is more than a matrix structure. It must be reinforced by matrix systems such as dual control and evaluation systems, by leaders who operate comfortably with lateral decision making, and by a culture that can negotiate open conflict and a balance of power."[15] Thus, the mere adoption of a matrix structure does not create a matrix organization.

Adoption must be followed by some fundamental changes in technical systems and management behavior. Managers must recognize the need to resolve issues and choices at the lowest possible level, without referring them to higher authority. A delicate balance of power must be maintained among managers facing each other. A tilt in favor of one organizational dimension or another would cause the organization to fall back to the old single-dimension vertical hierarchy, with the resulting loss of the benefits of the matrix structure. Absence of cooperation between facing managers, even when a perfect power balance exists, could cause so many unresolved problems and disputes to be referred up the hierarchy that top management would become overloaded with interdivisional matters.

The benefits of the matrix structure flow directly from the conditions that induce enterprises to adopt it. The organization can respond simultaneously to all environmental factors that are critical to its success. Decision-making authority can be decentralized to the appropriate level. Policy decisions are made in concert with people who have the relevant information, and the design facilitates the flow of information that promotes better planning and implementation of plans.

The matrix structure does take time, effort, and commitment by executives to make it work. Although Peter Drucker says that it "will never be a preferred form of organization; it is fiendishly difficult,"[16] he still concludes that "any manager in a multinational business will have to learn to understand it if he wants to function effectively himself."[17]

SUMMARY

This chapter was concerned with the typical stages in the evolution of the basic structures of international companies. Six organizational patterns were discussed: preinternational division phase; international division structure; global product division structure; global area structure; global functional structure; and the multidimensional global structure. The reasons for the adoption of each of these organizational types, as well as the advantages and disadvantages of each, were explained.

Finding the organizational structure most suited to the company's global corporate strategy is a challenge that a multinational company's top management executives must meet effectively and efficiently. The imperative to coordinate the three dimensions—function, product, and area—has created problems and tensions in the internal transactions and management of multinational companies. Companies usually modify the structures and make tradeoffs between the various approaches while attempting to integrate their geographically farflung operations.

Another challenge facing multinational company managers is that, after finding a suitable structure for a particular global corporate strategy at a certain point in time, they must keep modifying the structure to suit the evolving company strategy as well. This requirement for change will be ever present in multinational enterprises.

QUESTIONS

1. Discuss the salient features of the international division structure. What factors are responsible for its adoption by an international company?

2. How does the global product division differ from the global area division? What conditions favor the adoption of these structures?

3. Why is the matrix structure adopted by multinational companies? What are the advantages of the matrix structure? What conditions must accompany the adoption of the matrix in order for it to be successful in an organization?

FURTHER READING

1. Business International. *Organizing the Worldwide Corporation*, Research Report No. 69-4. New York: Business International, 1970.

2. Clee, Gilbert H., and Sachtjan, Wilbur M. "Organizing a Worldwide Business." *Harvard Business Review* 42, no. 6. (November–December 1964).

3. Davis, Stanley M. "Trends in the Organization of Multinational Corporations." *Columbia Journal of World Business*, Summer 1976.

4. Davis, Stanley. *Managing and Organizing Multinational Corporations*. New York: Pergamon Press, 1979.

5. Davis, Stanley M., and Lawrence, Paul R. "Problems of Matrix Organizations." *Harvard Business Review*, May–June 1978.

6. Drucker, Peter. *Management: Tasks, Responsibilities, Practices*. New York: Harper & Row, 1974.

7. Duerr, Michael G., and Roach, John M. *Organization and Control of International Operations*. New York: The Conference Board, 1973.

8. Goggin, William C. "How the Multidimensional Structure Works at Dow Corning." *Harvard Business Review*, January–February 1974.

9. Phatak, Arvind V. *Managing Multinational Corporations*. New York: Praeger Publishers, 1974.

10. Stopfard, John M., and Walls, Louis T., Jr. *Managing the Multinational Enterprise.* New York: Basic Books, 1972.
11. Vernon, Raymond, and Wells, Louis T., Jr. *Manager in the International Economy,* 4th ed. Englewood Cliffs, N.J.: Prentice-Hall, 1981.

NOTES

1. Raymond Vernon and Louis T. Wells, Jr., *Manager in the International Economy,* 3d ed. (Englewood Cliffs, N.J.: Prentice-Hall, 1976), p. 31.
2. Michael G. Duerr and John M. Roach, *Organization and Control of International Operations* (New York: The Conference Board, 1973), p. 5.
3. Stanley Davis, "Basic Structures of Multinational Corporations," in *Managing and Organizing Multinational Corporations,* ed. Stanley Davis (New York: Pergamon Press, 1979), p. 202.
4. Gilbert H. Clee and Wilbur M. Sachtjan, "Organizing a Worldwide Business," *Harvard Business Review* 42, no. 6 (November–December 1964): 60.
5. Business International, *Organizing the Worldwide Corporation,* Research Report No. 69–4 (New York: Business International, 1970), p. 9.
6. John M. Stopford and Louis T. Wells, Jr., *Managing the Multinational Enterprise* (New York: Basic Books, 1972), p. 51.
7. Stanley M. Davis, "Trends in the Organization of Multinational Corporations," *Columbia Journal of World Business,* Summer 1976, p. 60.
8. Davis, "Basic Structures," p. 203.
9. Ibid., p. 205.
10. Arvind V. Phatak, *Managing Multinational Corporations* (New York: Praeger Publishers, 1974), p. 183.
11. Duerr and Roach, *Organization and Control,* p. 12.
12. Ibid., p. 10.
13. Davis, "Trends in the Organization," p. 66.
14. Stopford and Wells, *Managing the Multinational Enterprise,* p. 87.
15. Stanley M. Davis and Paul R. Lawrence, "Problems of Matrix Organizations," *Harvard Business Review,* May–June, 1978, p. 4.
16. Peter Drucker, *Management: Tasks, Responsibilities, Practices* (New York: Harper & Row, 1974), p. 598.
17. Ibid.

Chapter **5**

International Staffing

In this chapter we shall consider the international staffing process. As the international business involvement of a company increases, so too does its need for well-qualified executives who are willing and able to be managers abroad. Not everyone who has been successful as a manager in one country can be as successful in another: it takes a person with a unique set of characteristics to succeed as a manager in diverse foreign environments.

Many costly managerial failures abroad can be avoided by the use of effective selection methods and predeparture training programs. Frequently, good managers who are also good candidates refuse to go abroad on managerial assignments because they fear that a foreign stint might have a negative impact on their career paths; to eliminate this problem, companies need a planned and communicable program for the repatriation of the manager who serves abroad.

A sound international executive compensation program is another essential component of an international staffing program. Thus, we shall examine in this chapter the main features of compensation for foreign assignment.

SOURCES OF MANAGERS

There are three main sources from which managers can be recruited to fill positions in the headquarters and in the foreign subsidiaries. They are the home country nationals; the host country nationals; and the third country nationals. Home (or parent) country nationals are the citizens of the country in which the headquarters of the multinational company is based. Citizens of the country that is hosting a foreign subsidiary are the host country nationals. Third country nationals are the citizens of a country other than the parent or the host country—for example a French executive working in a German subsidiary of an American multinational company. Most multinational corporations use all three sources for staffing their international operations, although some companies exhibit a distinct bias for one of the three types.

Home Country Nationals as Managers

Historically, multinational companies have had the tendency to staff the key positions in their foreign affiliates with home country nationals. Some classic reasons include: the unavailability of host country nationals having the required technical expertise; the desire to provide the company's more promising managers with international experience to equip them better for more responsible positions; the need to maintain and facilitate organizational coordination and control; the unavailability of managerial talent in the host country; the company's view of the foreign operation as short lived; the host country's multiracial population, which might mean that selecting a manager of either race would result in political or social problems; the company's conviction that it must maintain a foreign image in the host country; and the belief of some companies that a home country manager is the best person for the job.[1]

Research has shown that the most important motives for staffing foreign subsidiary management positions with home country nationals are these: (1) their technical expertise; and (2) during the start-up phase it is considered advantageous to have them there.[2] In a newly acquired subsidiary, the desire to ensure that the foreign subsidiary complies with the overall company objectives and policies induces the headquarters to staff it at the top with a home country national.

Third Country Nationals as Managers

Although the data on third country nationals are not as extensive as those on the home and host country nationals, the main advantages for using them are their technical expertise and the belief that the third country national is the best man for the job.[3]

U.S. corporations tend to use third country nationals only from advanced countries. The selection criteria for third country nationals are identical to those applied in the selection of home country nationals for foreign assignments; but the company's final objective for the two types of international managers is often different: in the case of the home country manager, most often the objective is to train and develop him for a top management position in the parent company headquarters. But for a third country national, a top management position at the subsidiary is usually envisioned as the ultimate in career development.

There are advantages and disadvantages in employing third country nationals. One advantage is that the salary and benefit requirements of the third country national may be significantly less than those of home country nationals. However, the salary scales for the two groups are approaching parity—reflecting the rapidly evolving management salary structure in many industrialized countries, particularly those of Western Europe. This equalizing trend applies particularly to third country nationals working in regional or international division headquarters.[4]

Another advantage of the third country national is that she or he may be better informed about the host environment. For example, the candidate may speak the host country's language—for example, a Belgian could work in France easily because French is the language spoken in both countries. Or a candidate's country may have a special relationship with the nation in which the subsidiary is located; thus a French citizen could adapt fairly readily to working in the Ivory Coast. For these reasons, many American companies have hired English or Scottish executives for top management positions in their subsidiaries in countries that were former British colonies—such as Jamaica, India, and Kenya.

Two distinct drawbacks may arise form the use of third country nationals. First, in certain parts of the world, animosities of national character exist between neighboring countries—for example, India and Pakistan, Greece and Turkey. Transfers of third country nationals must take such factors into account because an oversight in this area could be disastrous. The second disadvantage is associated with the desire of the governments of developing countries to upgrade their own people into responsible managerial positions. It is often more palatable to these governments to accept a home country national than to accept a third country national, even though the third country national might be better qualified for the position.

Host Country Nationals as Managers

Most multinational corporations use host country nationals in middle- and lower-level management positions in their foreign subsidiaries located in developing countries. This may be because the local law requires that they do so. But, perhaps the corporation would fill all managerial positions with host country nationals if there were not a scarcity of managers with the necessary qualifications for top jobs. In any event, it would be very difficult to staff the numerous middle-level positions totally with foreigners even if the local legislation permitted it.

When it comes to top management positions, the picture is not clear. Massey-Ferguson's Thornbrough asserts that "for all the talk, some North American companies still have the specific, rigid policy that key people in units abroad must be American."[5] This charge is refuted by a number of executives in other companies. The assistant general manager of the International Department at DuPont, David Cronklin, states: "Nationals head about half of our wholly owned subsidiaries in Europe and in only three of our eleven Latin-American subsidiaries are there American top executives on a long-term basis."[6] George Young, who is vice-president for international operations at Abbott Laboratories, says: "Abbot starts out by hiring [host country] nationals for foreign operations. Second choice is third-country nationals. Third preference is Americans. Out of 5000 employees overseas there are maybe three or four Americans at most."[7]

An important factor in determining to what extent host country nationals are selected for management positions is the increasing pressure by some governments for foreign firms to expedite the "nativization" of management. This pressure takes the form of sophisticated government persuasion through administrative or legislative decrees. For example, Brazil requires that two-thirds of the employees in a Brazilian subsidiary be Brazilian nationals; and there are pressures on multinationals to staff the upper management positions in Brazilian subsidiaries with

Brazilian nationals. In response to such pressure, many multinational corporations are subscribing to a policy similar to that described by a Standard Oil Company executive:

> While in the past we did employ substantial numbers of people for assignment overseas on a career basis, today, in keeping with our policy of utilizing nationals of the host country to the maximum extent possible, our practice is to assign domestic North American employees on relatively short-term transfer or loan basis.[8]

Research by Rosalie Tung on U.S. multinational corporations throws more light on the staffing of foreign subsidiaries. She found that U.S. multinational corporations have a tendency to use host country nationals at all levels of management to a much greater extent in the more advanced regions of the world than in the less advanced regions. This may be understandable, considering that the advanced countries are more likely to have a large pool of trained personnel with the necessary qualifications to occupy the managerial positions. The executives in the survey said that the most important reasons for hiring host country nationals were: (1) their familiarity with the local culture and language; (2) the lower costs incurred in hiring them as compared to the home or third country nationals; and (3) the improved public relations that resulted from such a practice.[9]

There are other reasons as well for the hiring of host country nationals to manage foreign subsidiaries. For instance, host country managers are believed to be more effective in dealing with local employees and clients than their foreign counterparts because they adhere to local patterns of management. There is also greater continuity of management because host country nationals tend to stay longer in their positions than managers from other countries. But more important is the avoidance of low morale that results when host country managers are not given opportunities to move into upper management positions. The following argument by an Italian manager in a U.S. multinational company's subsidiary in Italy illustrates this point:

> We feel we are the hurt and wounded part of Italian management. In an earlier time having . . . [Americans] here as managers was a good idea. As we have now developed our own management skills, some of those early advantages have disappeared. The right philosophy hasn't taken hold. . . . [and] the long hand of the parent is now a bad idea. I insist we who have been in the company ten, fifteen, or more years should have as much of the parent's confidence as do American managers. They some-

times come in here in fact for the . . . reason of stopping in Italy as birds of passage on their way to brilliant careers with the parent.[10]

What Are the Trends in International Staffing

Is there any pattern that can be detected in the international staffing practices of international companies? Research on this subject shows that changes in the international staffing policies tend to coincide with predictable stages of internationalization of multinational corporations. It appears, however, that the issue of nationality mix in multinational companies has received surprisingly little attention from researchers in the field of international management. Descriptions of when, where, and why firms use native or imported managerial personnel are generally found only in company histories. Some of the best research on international staffing involving U.S. and European companies has been conducted by Franko;[11] it revealed that in the first stage of internationalization, exports, most companies preferred to hire host country nationals because their greatest need was to adapt to local conditions, so local nationals were the logical choice. However, as the local market became large enough to support local manufacture of the product, home country managers were sent abroad during the first few years of the foreign manufacturing operation. After the start-up stage, the U.S. companies replaced home country (American) nationals by host country nationals. But in European companies the home country managers remained in the top foreign subsidiary positions, with many staying in the same country for the remainder of their working careers.

Franko did find, however, that American managers were often in charge of subsidiaries in those U.S. multinational corporations that followed a strategy of spreading a limited product line around the globe. As the limited product lines matured in successive markets, and as adaptation to local markets was replaced by a strategy of multinational product standardization, these firms pulled together the once relatively independent subsidiaries under the umbrella of a regional headquarters office. Then, U.S. managers were appointed both to head the regional divisions and to replace the host country nationals as subsidiary chiefs. European companies have also followed these trends in their staffing practices: they too placed home country managers in charge of the regional divisions and the subsidiaries.

As the process of rationalization was completed and as products and policies were standardized supranationally, the host country managers again replaced the home country managers as senior staff of local subsidiaries in U.S. firms; and some even filled the top managerial posts at the regional division headquarters. Some host country managers were also used to manage subsidiaries in third countries.

These findings from Franko's study are based on interviews and questionnaire responses from 25 European and U.S. firms, as well as from a survey of literature convering about 60 European and 170 U.S. companies with manufacturing operations in seven or more countries. Clearly, one cannot arrive at definite conclusions about the international staffing policies and practices on such a small sample. More research must be done in this area. However, one cannot discount the trends revealed by Franko's work.

Foreign Managers at Headquarters in Home Countries

More recently, foreign nationals have also come to occupy managerial jobs in the headquarters of U.S. and European multinational companies. Still, this is a rare occurrence. Multinationalization of headquarters management is a phenomenon that is taking place almost exclusively in the most mature industries and companies,[12] and in product areas with many years of international experience—such as oil, food processing, toiletries, synthetic fibers, and heavy electrical machinery.[13] It appears that the causes for this phenomenon are related to:

1. Horizontal mergers among competitors;
2. The nearly worldwide diffusion of skills in such industries;
3. The need for old firms in competitive industries to provide jobs "up the ladder" to foreign managers who could now leave to join competitors;
4. The possibility of political pressures from foreign governments who feel that competent local managers are now available."[14]

Some executives claim that the reason that they do not have foreigners at headquarters is that many do not want to come to work at the headquarters because of language barriers and strong roots in their own country. This may be true in some cases, but the real problem, says Howard Perlmutter, is "that U.S. companies prefer U.S. executives, because they trust them more. They speak the language of corporate headquarters."[15]

CRITERIA FOR SELECTING MANAGERS FOR FOREIGN ASSIGNMENTS

One of the most important factors in determining the success of a foreign operation—be it a branch or a fully integrated manufacturing subsidiary—is the quality of the home country managers sent abroad to manage it. This is particularly true during the start-up phase of the foreign operation.

The problem facing multinational companies is finding a manager who can readily adapt to the demands of a foreign assignment. There do not exist as yet valid and reliable screening devices to identify, with certainty, managers who will succeed in a foreign assignment. What we do have are the set of criteria which a manager should be able to meet before he or she can be even be considered for an assignment in a foreign country. Both home country and third-country managers are expatriates (though willingly); hence, the criteria we do have should apply in the selection of candidates from either of these two groups.

What are the ideal characteristics of an international manager? Following is one opinion on the subject:

> Ideally, it seems, he [or she] should have the stamina of an Olympic swimmer, the mental agility of an Einstein, the conversational skill of a professor of languages, the detachment of a judge, the tact of a diplomat, and the perseverance of an Egyptian pyramid builder. . . . And if he is going to measure up to the demands of living and working in a foreign country he should also have a feeling for culture; his moral judgements should not be too rigid; he should be able to merge with the local environment with chameleon-like ease; and he should show no signs of prejudice.[16]

Of course, that is an idealized profile of what an international manager should be. There are, however, several more realistic traits or characteristics which most personnel executives would agree a candidate must possess if he or she is to succeed at an assignment abroad. Having some or most of these characteristics does not ensure success, but the lack of them vastly increases the chances of failure. The paragraphs following take up some of these desirable traits.

Technical Ability

Obviously the candidate must have the technical knowledge and skills to do the job. Even though she or he may have each of the other attributes, if the candidate does not know what he or she is doing, there will be problems.

Managerial Skills

The candidate must know what it takes to be an effective manager. He or she must have the knowledge of the art and science of management and the ability to put it into practice. A good indicator of a candidate's managerial ability is her or his past record as a manager. Someone who has not been an effective manager in the home setting is not likely to be successful abroad.

Cultural Empathy

All authorities agree that high on the list of desirable traits is *cultural empathy*—which refers to "an awareness of and a willingness to probe for the reasons people of another culture behave the way they do."[17] It is critical for success abroad that the candidate be sensitive to cultural differences and similarities between his or her own home country and the host country. "He must have a personal philosophy that accepts value differences in other people and the ability to understand the inner logic and rationale of other people's way of life. He must be tolerant towards foreign cultural patterns and avoid judging others by his own values and criteria."[18] If one has cultural empathy, that person will demonstrate "an openness to experience, a willingness to respond realistically to relevant cues; a lack of dogmatism and a capacity for responding to the world, flexibly and dynamically."[19] Cultural empathy is undoubtedly a very desirable trait, even though it is difficult to identify in a candidate.

Adaptability and Flexibility

The ability to adapt to new circumstances and situations and to respond flexibly to different and often strange ideas and viewpoints is a characteristic found in successful international managers. The following are some specific types of adaptability and flexibility—listed originally in an American Management Association's research study—that an international manager should be capable of:

1. A high degree of ability to integrate with other people, with other cultures, and with other types of business operations.

2. Adaptability to change: being able to sense developments in the host country; recognizing differences, being able to evaluate them, and being able to qualitatively and quantitatively express the factors affecting the operations with which he is entrusted.

3. Ability to solve problems within different frameworks and from different perspectives.

4. Sensitivity to the fine print of differences in culture, politics, religion, and ethics, in addition to industrial differences.

5. Flexibility in managing operations on a continuous basis, despite lack of assistance and gaps in information rationale."[20]

All of the preceding items imply that there is a close association between cultural empathy and the manager's capacity to be adaptable and flexible. The candidate who lacks cultural empathy will find it extremely difficult to be adaptable and flexible in a foreign environment.

Diplomatic Skills

An international manager must be skilled in dealing with others. He or she must be able to represent the parent company in a foreign country as its ambassador—and be effective in advocating the parent company's point of view to foreign businesspersons, government bureaucrats, and poltical leaders. The manager should be a skilled negotiator, particularly in obtaining the most favorable treatment for the foreign subsidiary possible from the host country government. Diplomatic skills are particularly important in all countries where the manager has to interact often with politicians and government officials; but they are especially crucial in the developing nations of Asia, Africa, and Latin America, in which the role of the government in managing the business sector is quite significant.

Language Aptitude

The ability to learn a foreign language quickly can be quite an asset for an international executive. It is possible that the foreign assignment

may be in a country where one can get by with English; this is true of all countries that were once British colonies—for example, India, Kenya, Uganda, Guyana, Singapore, and Malaysia. However, the assignment may be to a country where English is not understood, in which case an aptitude in foreign languages could be of tremendous benefit.

Personal Motives

A candidate for an international assignment should have positive reasons for seeking it. Many persons apply for a foreign assignment because they believe that the higher salaries paid to international managers would make them rich quickly. A candidate who has this as the primary motive is not likely to be effective abroad unless she or he also has the other attributes discussed above.

The candidate's history is a good indicator of his or her interest in foreign countries and cultures and of his or her preparation for a foreign assignment: has she or he studied foreign languages, taken courses in international business, spent some years in the Peace Corps, or traveled or lived abroad for extended time periods?

Emotional Stability and Maturity

The emotional stability of a candidate has a direct bearing on that person's ability to survive in another culture. An emotionally stable person is one who is not subject to wide swings in mood. He or she does not get overly elated when good things happen, nor lapse into a depression when things do not go well. This person maintains emotional equilibrium at all times and is therefore able to cope constructively with adversity and to function day to day in various kinds of situations without being thrown off balance.

Emotional stability is a corollary of emotional maturity. The less judgmental a person is in his or her relationships with others, the more understanding she or he is of others and their perspective. The emotionally mature person is not likely to consider his or her way of doing things or behaving as the best way. An emotionally mature person is most likely to be emotionally stable as well.

Adaptability of Family

The ability of a manager to be effective in a foreign subsidiary depends to large extent upon how happy the manager's spouse and children are in the foreign environment. It is not always easy for a manager's family to feel comfortable in a country in which so many things are different from those at home. For example a family from the United States placed in Sri Lanka will find that the people look different, talk a strange language, eat spicy food, and dress differently; even the trees and shrubs, animals, birds, and insects are strange. To be transported to such an environment can be quite unsettling. The family might well get homesick for people at home and familiar surroundings. An unhappy family takes its toll on the effectiveness of the manager at work. The following account illustrates this problem:

> Some years ago, we chose a promising young man for a post in Nigeria. We were sure he was suited for the job. But the man had a family—two small children and a wife who had never been west of Pittsburgh. When they arrived in Nigeria that young wife from Montclair discovered how big insects are in Lagos. Three weeks later we brought the family home at a cost of almost $15,000.[21]

Here is another example to illustrate the problem that nonadaptability of the family can create for a company:

> Several years ago a U.S. engineering company ran into trouble while working on a steel mill in Italy. The crisis stemmed neither from inexperienced Italian personnel nor from volatile Italian politics but from the inability of an American executive's wife to adapt to Italy. Frustrated by language, schooling, and shopping problems, she complained incessantly to other company wives, who began to feel that they, too, suffered hardships and started complaining to their husbands. Morale got so bad that the company missed deadlines and, eventually, replaced almost every American on the job.[22]

What these examples imply is that no matter how gifted, competent, and suited the manager may be to work in a foreign country, that person's effectiveness as a manager will depend on the degree to which his or her family, and especially the spouse, adjusts to the foreign country's environment. A manager cannot perform at the peak of her or his abilities if his or her family is unhappy and yearning to go back home.

The preceding criteria are all important in selecting a manager for a foreign assignment. But what criteria do companies actually use in their selection process? A study by Rosalie Tung classified overseas managerial assignments into four categories:

1. The chief executive officer, who is responsible for the entire foreign operation;

2. The functional head, who is assigned the job of establishing functional departments in a foreign subsidiary;

3. The trouble shooter, who analyzes and solves specific operational problems; and

4. The operative.

Tung was interested in finding out whether the criteria used for selecting foreign personnel were contingent on the nature of the job they were expected to perform, the duration of stay in a foreign country, and the degree of contact with the local culture that the job entails. For instance, the chief executive officer would normally have greater contact with the local community and a longer length of stay abroad then would a troubleshooter.

Tung found that U.S. multinational corporations consider the most important criteria for the selection of the chief executive officer of a foreign subsidiary to be these: communication skills; managerial talent; maturity; emotional stability; and adaptability to new environmental settings. For the category of functional head, the most important criteria were maturity; emotional stability; and technical knowledge of the business—along with the same criteria as would be required for the same jobs at home. Technical knowledge of the business, initiative, and creativity were the criteria most important in the selection of a troubleshooter. And in the selection of an operative, the criteria considered to be most important were maturity, emotional stability, and respect of laws and people of the host country.[23]

SELECTION METHODS FOR FOREIGN ASSIGNMENTS

Once the company executives agree on the attributes that a candidate must possess as prerequisites for a foreign assignment, the next step is determining who among the available candidates has these attributes. Selection methods that companies use include: (1) examination of past performance, (2) battery of tests, and (3) extensive interviews.

Although it is generally accepted that past performance is not a sure indicator of future managerial success abroad because of the greatly different circumstances in which the manager has to work in a foreign country, most executives do examine the work history of a candidate. The purpose of looking into a candidate's past performance is to weed out those who are clearly not suited for greater responsibilities—on the assumption that those who have not done well at home are not likely to succeed abroad.

Some companies like to use a battery of tests to determine the candidate's technical ability and psychological suitability; they seek to determine how a candidate measures up on the various desirable attributes discussed earlier, such as adaptability, emotional stability and maturity, etc. However, not all companies are convinced that tests are useful as screening devices, so some choose to use them but not rely heavily on them; and others do not use them at all.

There is widespread agreement that extensive interviews of candidates and their wives or husbands by senior executives is by far the best method available for obtaining the necessary information in the selection process. In-depth interviews are conducted with the candidate to determine suitability for an assignment abroad. The kinds of questions for which answers are sought are:

1. Why does the candidate want to be considered for a foreign assignment?

2. How keen is he [or she] about getting a posting abroad?

3. Does the candidate have a realistic perspective of the opportunities, problems, and risks involved in living and working abroad?

4. Is there evidence that the candidate is self-reliant, adaptable, and able to work independently? ·

5. What evidence is there that the candidate can learn foreign languages quickly?

6. Has he made career moves in the U.S. successfully?

7. Does he or his family have any medical problems?

8. How many children does he have and how old are they? Will the children move or stay back home?

9. How enthusiastic is each member of the family about staying abroad?

These questions are just a few of the many that executives may ask in trying to determine how qualified the candidate is for a foreign posting.

Recognizing the importance of assessing the ability of the executives and their families to adjust to life abroad, a growing number of companies are adopting a technique called adaptability screening.[24] The program is conducted either by a professional psychologist or psychiatrist on the company's staff or by a personnel director trained in the technique. Two factors are generally measured during the screening: the family's success in handling transfers in the United States and its reactions to discussions of stresses that the transfer abroad and life in a particular foreign country may cause. The interviewer tries to alert the couple to personal issues involved in a transfer. For instance, the couple may have an aging, widowed, or ailing parent or close relative whom they may have to leave behind; they are told they may feel guilty and anxious. Or the family might have strong bonds to their church or civic organizations. Such strong bonds could cause stresses after the family is physically separated from people and activities that are important to it. The frustrations of adjusting to a strange culture and learning to communicate in a new language are also highlighted during the interview.

The objective of adaptability screening is to make the family aware of the different types of potential stresses and crisis that could arise in a transfer abroad, and to prevent a failure abroad by giving the family a chance to say no to the transfer before it takes place. It costs anywhere from $20,000 to $30,000 to move a family abroad, hence, it is far more cost effective to prevent a bad transfer than it is to send a family abroad only to have it request a transfer back home again. In addition to alerting the family, the screening interview also permits the interviewer to assess the family's suitability for a stint overseas; there have been times when the family wants to go abroad but the interviewer kills the transfer.

PREPARING MANAGERS FOR FOREIGN ASSIGNMENTS

Once a manager is selected for a foreign assignment, it is in the best interests of the company to ensure that this person and his or her family are prepared to handle the foreign assignment as effectively as possible. This goal may be met by having the family group attend a well-planned predeparture training program. Such a training program has the following two principal objectives: One, to make it easier for the manager to assume her or his responsibilities and be effective on the job in the foreign environment as soon as possible; and two, to facilitate the adaptation of the manager and family to the foreign culture, with the fewest problems. The best program will probably have two phases. The executive alone should be involved in the first phase of the program, and both the executive and family should be included in phase two.

For the Manager

Phase one of the program, which is for just the executive, should include study and discussion of at least the following elements:

- Characteristics of the economy, political structure, political stability, and legal environment of the host country.
- Relationship between the subsidiary and the rest of the company. The extent to which the subsidiary's operations are interlocked with the operations of other subsidiaries and of the parent company.
- The economic and political aspirations of the host country as reflected in the government's policies, and what it expects of the subsidiary in areas such as creation of more jobs, exports, development of local resources, etc.
- Management practices peculiar to the host country (for example, the practice of permanent employment and consensual decision making, both of which are typical of Japanese management).
- A comprehensive job description, which specifies the authority, responsibilities, duties, and tasks of the manager's position in the foreign subsidiary.
- The overall objectives and goals the manager is expected to achieve.

For the Manager and Family

Phase two of the program, which includes the executive and family, should focus on helping the participants to adapt to the foreign environment as effectively and quickly as possible. To achieve this goal, the program should at least have the following elements: (1) language training, (2) area study, and (3) cross-cultural training.

Language Training

Language training is a must for the entire family. It gives them a start on becoming acclimated to their new country. The goal of language training is to provide the family with an elementary knowledge of the vocabulary so that they may be able to communicate with others on arrival in the host country. Simple things, such as ordering a meal in a restaurant, asking for directions, or reading street signs can be quite bewildering. Even a few hours of instruction prior to departure—even as little as 20 to 30 hours—can make a tremendous difference, and will provide the family with the very basic vocabulary required to get started.[25]

Area Study

This element of training includes an intensive study of the host country's culture, politics, geography, climate, food, currency, and attitude towards foreigners. The family may be given books to read on this subject. Lectures by area experts, accompanied by film presentations, have been found to be useful because they give the participants the opportunity to ask the experts questions on specific areas of concern.

Cross-Cultural Training

This training has as its purpose the preparation of individuals to interact and communicate effectively in other cultures; individuals will learn how to work with people who think, behave, and perceive things differently, and who hold different beliefs and values. There are four basic models of cross-cultural training.[26]

The Intellectual Model. This training model consists of lectures and reading about the host country. The premise of this model is that factual knowledge about another culture should prepare an executive for living or working in that culture.

The Area Simulation Model. This is a program tailored to the specific culture in which the executive and her or his family will be immersed. Attempts are made to create a variety of situations that the participants are likely to face in the foreign culture. The idea is that exposure to these situations will teach the family how to function in the new culture.

The Self-Awareness Model. Programs based on this model have the premise that understanding oneself and why one behaves the way one does is critical to understanding other persons, particularly those of another culture. Sensitivity training is the main ingredient of this method.

The Cultural Awareness Model. This training technique assumes that for an individual to function successfully in another culture, he or she must first learn the universal principles of behavior, those that exist across cultures. The program attempts to make the participants aware of the influence of culture on an individual, and of how they differ from the peoples of other countries because of cultural differences. The focus of the program is on improving the participants' ability to recognize cultural influences in personal value, behaviors, and cognitions. This ability should enhance a person's skill at diagnosing difficulties in intercultural communication—and lower his or her inclination to make judgments when confronted with behavior that appears strange.

There are many different methods of cross-cultural training, such as the Cultural Assimilator or the Contrast-American Method of Cross-Cultural Training. It is beyond the scope of this chapter to discuss these techniques in detail, but we can say that, regardless of the type of method used, the objectives of all cross-cultural training programs are similar:

1. To encourage greater sensitivity and more astute observations in areas and situations, as well as people, who are culturally different.

2. To foster greater understanding in dealing with representatives of microcultures within one's own country.

3. To improve employee and customer relations by creating an awareness of cultural differences and their influence on behavior.

4. To develop more cosmopolitan organizational representatives who not only understand the concepts of culture, but can apply this knowledge to interpersonal relations and organizational culture.

5. To increase managerial effectiveness in international operations, especially with regard to cross-cultural control systems, negotiations, decision-making, customer relations, and other vital administration processes.

6. To improve cross-cultural skills of employees on overseas assignments, or representatives of microcultures in our own country.

7. To reduce culture shock when on foreign deployment, and to enhance the intercultural experience for employees.

8. To apply the behavioral sciences to international business and management.

9. To increase job effectiveness through training in human behavior, particularly in the area of managing cultural differences.

10. To improve employee skills as professional intercultural communicators.[27]

The cross-cultural training programs may be conducted by professionals who understand cross-cultural education and challenges. Such professionals may include psychologists; cultural anthropologists; communications specialists; and human resources development specialists, trainers, and facilitators. Nationals of the host country, third country nationals experienced in the particular culture, and local professors with relevant expertise can all be drafted to assist in such a program. There are management consulting organizations, universities, and agencies that specialize in cross-cultural education who may also be called upon for assistance.

Up until now we have been looking at the strategy an international company should implement to improve the chances of a manager's success in a foreign assignment. But executives at the parent company cannot sit back and assume that, having prepared the manager for the foreign posting, they have done their part and now it is up to the manager to perform. The manager abroad may experience many anxieties that are not related to the environment in the foreign country, but which emanate, rather, from his or her being physically and emotionally separated from the parent company. Such anxieties can have a very detrimental impact on job performance.

There are things that executives in the parent comany do—some before the manager's departure and some during her or his tenure abroad—to help alleviate the anxieties. We shall examine this subject in the following section.

REPATRIATING THE INTERNATIONAL MANAGER

A problem that has become of increasing concern to both the managers abroad and their companies is the reentry of the managers into their home country organizations. Most expatriates take the foreign assignments for several years, under the assumption that they will eventually return to their home country, either to headquarters or to a subsidiary in the home country. More often than not, this move back home is a source of potential anxiety for the manager.

What are the reasons for the anxiety of returning home? Among the foremost reasons is the fear that the company has not planned adequately for this person's return; perhaps he or she will be placed temporarily—which may mean many months—in a mediocre or makeshift job.[28] There is also the anxiety that an extended foreign stay may have caused the manager a loss of visibility and isolation from the parent company, which may have an adverse effect upon the manager's career and upward mobility in the organization. The expatriate manager is anxious that, despite the access to the formal power structure he or she had from the foreign post a manager abroad still loses contact with the informal power structure within the company.[29] There is the apprehension, too, that she or he may miss opportunities for advancement at home, and that peers would be promoted ahead of him or her.

Another source of anxiety is the possibility of failure in the foreign assignment and its impact upon a once-promising career. If a manager fails at her or his foreign assignment, he or she is usually penalized indirectly by the company's attitude, which looks with disfavor upon such failures. This attitude is exemplified in the following comment by the director of employee relations of Dow Chemical, U.S.A.: "If a person flunks out overseas . . . we bring him home. . . . He's penalized indirectly because the odds are that if he flunked out over there, he's in trouble over here. But we bring him back and, generally, he has a tough row to hoe." [30] This attitude is neither fair nor logical, considering that the challenge of the type of problems, both work-related and personal, and of the environment to an expatriate manager is very different—and usually more difficult—than what faces the domestic counterpart of this manager.

Getting used to working under organizational constraints may be hard for some expatriates when they come back home. Abroad, the manager had a lot more autonomy; physical distance from the parent company permitted the manager to function independently and to demonstrate what she or he could accomplish without much corporate assistance. When the manager returns home, even if it means coming back to a bigger job in the organizational hierarchy, he or she still must operate as a member of an organization that constrains the freedom to act: "One minute he is Patton roaring across the desert . . . and the next he is on Eisenhower's staff where the moves must be made an inch at a time." [31]

A sense of a loss of status may be also experienced by the executive upon coming home. Abroad, especially for a local general manager or senior executive, the manager was probably a very prominent member in the local community. Back home she or he is apt to be just another executive.

An expatriate manager may have to incur financial burdens when he or she returns. For instance the returning manager may find that he or she no longer can afford to buy a home similar to the one sold a few years before. In addition, the abundant benefits and perquisites that she or he received as inducement to accept the foreign post are eliminated upon return. Even if promoted, the returning manager may in essence be taking a pay cut.

What can companies do to ease the reentry of expatriate managers? Some companies—such as Westinghouse Electric, Dow Chemical, and Union Carbide—use "repatriation agreements," written guarantees that a manager will not be kept abroad longer than two to five years and that, upon return, he or she will be placed in a job that is mutually acceptable. The written agreement does not promise the expatriate any promotion or specific salary increase upon return; in fact it may state that the manager may wind up in a job equal to, if not better than, the one he had abroad. Such repatriation agreements could be of great value in alleviating the career-related anxieties of expatriate managers.

Another strategy to ease repatriation is to make senior executives serve as sponsors of managers abroad. It is the responsibility of a sponsor to monitor the performance, compensation, and career paths of expatriate managers who are under their wings, and to plan for their return. Sponsors begin scouting anywhere from six months to a year prior to an expatriate's return for a suitable position that he or she can come back to.[32] Union Carbide and IBM are two companies who make use of such sponsors, but there are others as well. Dow Chemical has a cadre of ten full-time counselors who act as "godfathers" of the expatriates. Once a year they travel abroad to meet each of the foreign-based managers to explore and understand the manager's career goals and how any changes in such goals could be accommodated. The counselors also act as advocates for the managers back home to ensure that they are given due consideration for any promotional opportunities that may occur during their foreign stay.[33] Sponsors and counselors are helpful in keeping the expatriate manager in touch with developments at home, and they help to ease the career-oriented concerns of expatriates.

Other methods of keeping the expatriate manager plugged into the informal power structure include corporate management meetings around the world, regularly scheduled meetings at the headquarters, and combining home leave with an extended stay at the headquarters to work on specific problems or projects.[34]

To lessen the financial difficulties caused by inflation in the housing market, companies such as Aluminum Company of America and Union Carbide have established programs to rent or otherwise maintain an expatriate's home while she or he is away. Union Carbide pays real estate and legal fees to help most of its international executives rent their homes. Such a program can erase the problem an executive would otherwise face on returning home—finding that a home similar to the one he used to live in has become unaffordable!

THE HOST COUNTRY NATIONAL

It is not uncommon for host country governments to put restrictions on the employment of foreign nationals. Such restrictions reflect a desire to ensure full employment among their own work-force. These restrictions may appear to be unnecessary and inconvenient to the multinational corporation looking to utilize the best human resources available, but the multinational corporation must realize that, just as they are seeking to maximize the return on their investment, so is the host government. As a result of these requirements, it is becoming increasingly common for local nationals to rise to the top executive positions.

Advantages of Host Country Managers

The local manager does in fact have an advantage over an expatriate. Cultural differences may be difficult to overcome for the expatriate but the local manager, on the other hand, is very familar with the local environment, local businessmen, and government officials. In the area of public relations the local manager can be extremely helpful. Knowledge of local customs is essential for minimizing the inevitable bureaucratic red tape. In Latin America and Asia it is not uncommon for local officials to refuse to conduct business with anyone other than a local national of managerial status.[35]

The local manager helps to minimize any bad feelings the foreign government may have toward the multinational operation. A company having a responsible attitude toward the local community should alleviate many of the fears the local government might have. A company with a policy to train local nationals to assume greater responsibility within the corporation would be received enthusiastically and should have good relations with the local community.

Recruitment and Selection

Problems are often encountered by multinational corporations seeking to recruit and select local nationals for positions within the corporation.

Local customs and educational opportunities, particularly in under-developed countries, often produce individuals deficient in aptitudes traditionally regarded by Western management as essential to top management performance. Economic growth concepts and the role of capital, profits, savings, and investment are often misunderstood and unacceptable to those raised in developing countries. Consequently, the likelihood of finding suitable managerial candidates is reduced. This is not often a difficulty to the same degree in developed or industrialized countries.

Under the best of circumstances, finding acceptable local managers is a difficult and time-consuming assignment. There are four basic sources to choose from: the present workforce, local and foreign university graduates, government agencies, and local businesses. The first and most obvious place to look within an operating subsidiary is to the present workforce. Someone from the nonmanagement ranks or lower supervisory position may be prepared to assume greater responsibility.

Until the subsidiary is established, the executive search goes into the local business community. Local managers may feel that working for a foreign-owned organization poses certain threats; hence salary, fringe benefits, working conditions and advancement opportunities must be comparable to or better than those offered by other local firms. When strong nationalistic feelings are part of the culture, a local manager is viewed as a bit of an economic traitor. This is especially true when the firm is in competition with a national company. Conditions must be attractive enough to make the adjustment worthwhile.

Finding the right person for a specific job in a foreign subsidiary is not easy. Few local managers have the experience or training desired by the multinational. In addition, local managers are not accustomed to changing jobs with the same frequency as in the United States.

An effective selection interview must be tailored to the local culture. For instance, in many countries, questions regarding a person's family, hobbies, parents, or religious convictions are often considered unacceptable.[36] In general, these areas are private and not subject to questioning by a stranger. An effective interview must probe, instead, into the candidate's motivations, ambitions, communication abilities, and management style.

The multinational home management must keep in mind, too, that it is extremely difficult, if not impossible, to terminate an employee in most developing countries—where an employee is practically guaranteed a job for life.[37] Strong unions and government regulations restrict the company's actions when an employee proves unsuited for a given job.

Finally, the success of the local manager is necessary for the long-run success of the foreign subsidiary for it is ultimately the local manager who will replace the managers from the home country and third countries.

MULTINATIONAL STAFFING PHILOSOPHIES

The multinational staffing practices of a company are influenced significantly by the way top management executives at the head-quarters think about doing business around the world and particularly their orientation toward foreign executives in headquarters and subsidiaries. Howard Perlmutter has identified three primary attitudes among international executives that can be inferred from examining the mangerial practices of companies that have substantial foreign operations. He has labeled them as ethnocentric, polycentric, and geocentric.[38]

A multinational company of any country may exhibit ethnocentric, polycentric, or geocentric attitudes. In an ethnocentric corporation, the prevailing attitude is that home country attitudes, management style, knowledge, evaluation criteria, and managers are superior to anything the host country might have to offer. Consequently, top management executives at headquarters and at all subsidiaries are from the home country exclusively.

A polycentric corporation treats each of its subsidiaries as distinct national entities. There is a conscious belief that only host country managers can ever really understand the culture and behavior of the host country market; therefore, the foreign subsidiary should be managed by local people. However, no local manager can ever hope to be promoted to a position at headquarters, which is staffed exclusively with home country people.

The third attitude, which is still rarely observed today among multinational corporations, is geocentric. Geocentrism is based on the policy of searching for management candidates on a global basis. A geocentric philosophy of staffing must be accompanied by a worldwide integrated business philosophy to be successful. Thus, the selection and training of management at the international level must take place without regard to the managers' nationalities; thus, management potential from anywhere in the world can be employed to the advantage of the multinational company as a whole, wherever it is necessary, at headquarters as well as in the subsidiaries.

It is true that geocentrism is limited in some countries by legal and political factors. Despite this, it is very important for a company operating as a true multinational entity to have a personnel policy that is likewise multinational. In view of the demands on a multinational company's management, it is necessary to have an internationally employable "fire brigade." Also, because the environment of the multinational company is truly global, the result of multinational recruiting should be a cadre of top management at the headquarters—one that is not only internationally oriented but also composed of nationals of various countries.[39]

The feasibility of implementing a geocentric policy is based on five related assumptions:

1. Highly competent employees are available not only at headquarters, but also in the subsidiaries.

2. International experience is a condition for success in top positions.

3. Managers with high potential and ambition for promotion are constantly ready to be transferred from one country to another.

4. Competent and mobile managers have an open disposition and high adaptability to different conditions in their various assignments.

5. Those not blessed initially with an open disposition and high adaptability can acquire these qualities as their experience abroad accumulates.[40]

These five assumptions hold true in varying degrees, depending on a company's particular circumstances. And, in most cases, multinational firms with a truly global outlook realize the need to combine different nationalities in managing their operations. However, despite these beliefs and the desire to become geocentric, a large number of companies are still a long way from internationalizing their staff. There is usually still a strong emotional attachment to the enterprise's original country which reflects an attitude that the quality of management and also the cohesion of the organization requires at least a certain proportion of experienced men from the home country.[41] Nevertheless, ideally the goal of a company's international staffing policy should be a corporate pool of experienced international executives who are available for assignment wherever their skills are needed. In other words, to operate as a truly geocentric company, a multinational firm must have geocentric managers.

INTERNATIONAL EXECUTIVE COMPENSATION

If there is one area of multinational personnel policy that can be designated the most complex, it has to be the area of compensation. The problems to date defy a simple solution and cause much intraorganizational resentment. The basic compensation strategy of international companies is to pay a base salary and apply to it the base differentials determined by the country of location of the affiliate. The problems arise in determining the base salary, and in determining the type and amount of the differentials, and in deciding which countries they apply to. The following discussion covers some standard approaches developed by multinational companies to deal with compensation; as well as some methods of determining the salaries of home, host and third country nationals; and a review of the various differentials.

Evolution of Compensation Systems

The development of multinational compensation systems in effect today has been quite haphazard. The American businessman has been working abroad since this country began. In the early days, the manager received the same salary abroad that he would have received at home; there was no compensation for additional expenses. This policy fell apart when the oil companies started sending employees to the Middle East, where they were often obliged to live and work in primitive conditions. Consequently, they had a difficult time convincing qualified people to accept such positions. The idea of premium pay was then developed and other companies followed the lead. In those early days of premium pay, there was no set percentage allowed for foreign service; rather, the embarking employee negotiated the amount of his premium. Understandably, the resultant variation in pay for one company's employees working in the same country caused some discontent. The policy eventually evolved into a standard percentage for premium pay anywhere abroad; finally it became a premium designed to maintain the expatriate's "real" salary in his particular foreign post.[42]

Today expatriate compensation can roughly be categorized into three standard approaches. The first approach is based on *a headquarters scale plus affiliate differentials.* The base salary of the home country national is determined by what the salary for that job would be at headquarters. With many companies now using the balance sheet method of determining differentials, an affiliate differential can be a positive addition to the expatriate's salary, or it can be a negative allowance to account for any extra benefits associated with the particular foreign assignment. Under this system, the host country nationals are entitled neither to the base salary not the differentials allotted to home country nationals; rather, their salaries are based on local salary standards. The third country nationals pose a problem though. The company may either treat them as host country nationals or home country nationals; in either case, inequities are possible. This system is undoubtedly the most ethnocentric of the three.[43]

The citizenship salary system solves the problem of what to do about the third country national. An executive's regular salary is based on the standard for his country of citizenship or native residence. An appropriate affiliate differential is then added based on comparative factors between the executive's native country and his host country. This system works well as long as expatriates with similar positions do not come from countries with different salary scales. As affiliate staffing becomes more internationalized, it has become harder to avoid precisely this problem. Consequently, the inequities arising from different salary scales for the same position do not go unnoticed.[44]

The global compensation system is one move toward a more geocentric personnel policy, although it too has its constraints. Under this system, the same job has the same base salary, regardless of country. Affiliate differentials are then added to the base. Differentials are determined by affiliate location and job or rank, but are unrelated to the home country of the expatriate. The resultant system allows for no unexplained inequities between employees performing the same job in the same subsidiary. A prerequisite for this type of compensation scale is a global system of job classification. The task of measuring comparable job elements across cultural boundaries is awesome, and no company has completely succeeded in this respect. Nevertheless, efforts are being made in this direction, and the global salary structure seems surely to be the system of the future.[45]

Dealing with Dissatisfaction

Until the global salary system becomes a reality, most multinational companies are operating under one of the first two compensation systems. Under these systems, the most troublesome problem has been the host country national's salary. In the past, the remuneration of local nationals has been ruled by the local salary levels. This practice stems from the multinational companies' fear of raising the salary standards for the entire area and thus raising the affiliate's costs of operation. The pressure to utilize more native managers plus local statutory limitations on expatriate employment have increased the demand for capable host country nationals. The increased competition between companies with subsidiaries in the same country has led to a gradual upgrading of local manager's salaries.

One company has divided its employees into two classifications. If a local employee meets certain established performance standards, he is shifted from local management status to the international executive corps. His pay is then adjusted to the new, higher salary scale of the other international executives, including Americans. The promoted local manager, in turn, agrees to be available for transfer to any other country where his services may be needed.

Another approach is to shift all local managers above a certain level to the headquarters scale. Under this system junior and lower-middle management personnel may remain on a local salary standard, while the upper-level management is on a higher standard.

A third approach is to use management by objectives to determine local salary. While this system does not necessarily eliminate the difference between local and expatriate salaries, it does provide a more rational explanation for the difference. Overall, however, international firms are moving toward a narrowing of the salary gap between the host country national and the expatriate.[46]

As the number of third country nationals in multinational companies increases, their compensation level is also approaching that of the home country expatriate.[47] One of the problems peculiar to the third country national, however, is defining them. The most common definition is "one who works outside his home country for a company based in still another country.[48] But is a Frenchman working for a Spanish-based company in Geneva or an Argentine working for a U.S.–based firm in Santiago really an expatriate third country national? And why do most U.S.–based companies consider Canadian nationals working abroad as U.S. expatriates and not as third country nationals?[49] Some countries are using cultural zones rather than nations to define third country nationals. For example, Western Europe may be one zone; Africa, another; etc.[50] Other companies use a combination of geographic and language zones; thus an employee remains a local national (not a third country national) unless he moves to a different geographic zone and a different language zone as well.[51]

Salary Differentials

The final section of this discussion on compensation is a brief review of the different types of differentials. It is not meant to be an exhaustive examination of each area but simply an introduction to the different components and some of their problems.

The Overseas Premium (OP)

This differential is usually paid as a percentage of the executive's base salary. There are a number of reasons companies still use the OP, but three basic rationalizations emerge: (1) the executive is being compensated for the various emotional, cultural, and physical adjustments he or she will have to make; (2) the executive is being given an incentive to accept a foreign assignment; and (3) the company must offer an OP because its competitors are offering one.[52] Some sources feel the OP is practical since it indicates to the employee that the company realizes the inconvenience she or he is undergoing; the company avoids the administrative costs of analyzing and pricing each inconvenience separately; and the alternative would be to increase the base salary, distort the firm's salary structure, and increase the costs of pension and other salary-based expenditures.[53]

Many industrial relations specialists assert that paying the same flat percentage of base salary to the executive going from Peoria to the deserts of Saudi Arabia as that paid to the executive going from New York to Paris is preposterous, and a number of companies have considered eliminating or modifying their OP. One suggested modification has been the reduction of the OP over time; another is that the percentage should be based on the degree of contrast between the home country environment and host country environment.[54]

Reimbursement for Payments into Host Country Welfare Plans

Most developed countires require workers to contribute to some type of state welfare plan, whether it be pension, medical, or unemployment. Since the expatriate is almost always concurrently making payments in the United States to a pension fund (and any benefits accruing to him abroad will probably not be claimed), companies often leave the local payment to the expatriate and compensate for it in the cost of living allowance. This occurs particularly when the local tax regulations would treat the company's contribution to the host country program on behalf of an individual as a taxable fringe benefit. In the case of company pension plans, some companies "forgive" the employee's contributions while overseas. Where mandatory state medical plans exist, the company may reimburse the employee only for those expenses which are not provided free by the state.[55]

Housing Allowance

A housing allowance is provided by companies to permit the executive to maintain living accommodations comparable to what he had at home and also to house him in a fashion comparable to his foreign peers. Some companies simply pay the difference (or a portion of the difference) between normal housing costs at home and the cost of housing in the foreign country. The problem with this method is determining the cost of normal domestic housing. Another common approach is to require the employee to pay up to a certain percentage of his salary for housing, and the company is responsible for the difference. In these types of plans, the company may set a ceiling on the amount it will contribute to discourage excessively lavish choices of housing by the manager living abroad.[56]

Cost of Living (COL) Allowance

This differential is probably the most controversial of the differentials. Critics claim that a good international manager chooses to experience the novel conditions of a foreign lifestyle, and he and his family will eventually alter their consumption patterns and tastes to the foreign environment. By this reasoning, a COL allowance is not needed or, at least, can be decreased over time.

Proponents of the COL counter that an expatriate has the right to live in a foreign country as he does at home. In addition, maintaining a familiar lifestyle may be essential to the family's satisfaction with the foreign assignment. The biggest problem is determining cost of living indexes. The most easily available resource is the U.S. State Department's index; but it is often out of date and contains cultural biases. Many companies develop their own indexes or turn to a private research firm for one.[57]

Education and Perquisites

This allowance included schooling for children, club memberships, and home leave, among other amenities. Education is probably the most commonly provided expense, and policy is usually uniform among companies. The company attempts to provide the means whereby an expatriate can educate his children in their mother tongue up to the level required for university entrance in their home country, at a cost to him no greater than he would have had to bear at home. Implementation of this policy, particularly regarding transportation and determination of an acceptable school, varies according to the parent country and the local facilities.

Clubs are an essential feature of business life in some countries, and fees can be expensive. Some firms provide nothing for club membership; others pay the entrance fee but not the dues; very few pay all membership fees.

Home leave also varies between companies, but the most common policy is to grant thirty days home leave after eleven or twelve months abroad. The class of travel allowed is usually determined by the amount of time spent in the air (e.g., first class for a flight exceeding ten hours, tourist for a shorter journey).[58]

Income Taxes

This can be an extremely complex area of international compensation. In some countries, only locally paid compensation is taxable; but in most, worldwide compensation is taxable. U.S.-based companies tend to prefer tax equalization plans in which the company withholds from the employee his U.S. tax liability and pays his local taxes. British companies, on the other hand, vary their policy, depending on the affiliate country. The tax equalization policy presents the danger of paying multiple taxes; that is, in many countries a tax paid by a company on behalf of an employee is also taxable. It has been suggested that a company with operations in many countries would be better off adopting a tax equalization policy—it would gain in some countries while losing in others. But if the company operates in only a few countries, it would be best to leave the local taxes to the employee and adjust other local allowances accordingly.[59]

Fluctuations in Exchange Rates

The fluctuations between parent and host countries are provided for by the inclusion of a currency cushion in the overseas premium if the fluctuations are minor. Major currency changes are dealt with through special allowances. To avoid unnecessary problems and costs, local price reviews are sometimes delayed for six months after a major change; third country nationals are paid in home country currency; a proportion of the expatriate's salary is retained in his or her home country; and any special allowance is reduced over time.[60]

In conclusion, a good compensaion program must meet the needs of two groups: the corporation and its employees. "A multinational company that needs to widen its horizons to get the best managers regardless of citizenship must structure a salary plan equitable enough to compensate all managers fairly, and attractive enough to draw the top managers it needs."[61]

COMPENSATING THE HOST COUNTRY NATIONAL

In general, U.S. corporations have not offered local nationals compensation packages that are equal to those offered to home and third country expatriates. Local nationals are typically compensated in accordance with local standards, which means that the total compensation package of the local manager often amounts to as little as one-half or even one-third of that of an expatriate manager with identical credentials and doing essentially the same job.

In order to attract and retain high-quality local managers, multinational companies must ensure that the total compensation package is not only internally equitable but also externally competitive. The various components of the package must consider local conditions, such as the tax structure; cultural variables, such as status symbols; and governmentally legislated social welfare schemes, such as health insurance and pension plans. Consideration of such factors—which vary from country to country—would enable the company to design a compensation package for the local manager which is most beneficial to him in terms of the specific local conditions.

SUMMARY

International companies have three main sources from which they can draw their pool of international managers—the home country, the host country, and a third country. Home country nationals are the citizens of the country in which the headquarters of the company is located. Nationals of the country in which the foreign affiliate is situated are the host country nationals. Nationals of a country that is neither the home nor host country are the third country nationals. For instance, an Italian working in the French subsidiary of an American company would be classified as a third country national.

Multinational companies have a tendency to staff the key positions in their foreign affiliates with home country nationals. Third country nationals are also used frequently, but most companies prefer to use nationals of advanced countries in this capacity. Most multinationals use host country nationals in middle- and lower-level positions in the subsidiaries that are located in developing countries. In the more advanced countries, they employ host country nationals to a far greater extent at all levels of management. This is probably because more qualified personnel are available in the advanced countries than in the developing countries.

Recently, foreign nationals have been named to managerial positions in the headquarters of U.S. and European multinational corporations. However, this is still a rare occurrence.

Most personnel executives would agree that a candidate for a foreign assignment must possess a few key characteristics if he or she is to be successful abroad. Having these features does not ensure success, but not having them greatly increases the probability of failure. These characteristics are: technical ability, managerial skills, cultural empathy, adaptability and flexibility, diplomatic skills, language aptitude, personal motives, emotional stability and maturity, and adaptability of family. Selection methods used by companies to determine which candidates have these attributes include an examination of each candidate's past performance; battery of tests; and extensive interviews of the candidate and spouse.

The selected candidate should be put through a well-planned predeparture program, the purpose of which is not only to make the manager capable of assuming her or his new job abroad and be effective on it quickly, but also to facilitate the manager's own as well as his or her family's adaptation to the foreign culture. Companies should also have effective programs to facilitate the reentry of the expatriate manager into the home country organization at the completion of the foreign assignment.

Companies exhibit ethnocentric, polycentric, or geocentric staffing philosophies. Companies that have an ethnocentric staffing philosophy staff their foreign affiliates almost exclusively with home country nationals. Host country nationals are employed predominantly by those companies that have a polycentric philosophy. Companies with a geocentric staffing philosophy adopt the strategy of selecting and putting the right candidate in the right job, anywhere in the world, regardless of the nationality of the candidate.

Probably the most complex aspect in the international staffing area is the one concerned with international executive compensation. The basic compensation strategy of international companies is to pay a base salary and apply to it the base differentials contingent on the country of location of the affiliate.

QUESTIONS

1. "Changes in the international staffing policies tend to coincide with predictable stages of internationalization of multinational corporations." Discuss why.

2. Does the nature of the job and the length of the stay abroad influence the criteria for the selection of candidates for a foreign assignment? What are the traits that an international manager should possess if she or he were to be appointed as the chief executive of a foreign affiliate?

3. Why is the preparation of the manager and her or his family for a foreign assignment just as important as the selection of the right candidate? What should be the objective and essential features of a predeparture training program?

4. "Planning to bring an executive back home after a foreign assignment is as important as planning to send her or him abroad." Discuss.

5. How would you approach the problem of determining an equitable compensation package for an American and an Egyptian who have been assigned to work on similar jobs in the Japanese subsidiary of an American multinational company?

FURTHER READING

1. Borrman, W.A., "The Problem of Expatriate Personnel and Their Selection in International Enterprises." *Management International Review* no. 4–5, (1968).

2. *Compensating International Executives.* New York: Business International Corporation, 1970.

3. Crystal, Graef S. *Compensating U.S. Expatriates Abroad: An AMA Management Briefing.* New York: American Management Association, 1972.

4. Desatnick, R.L., and Bennett, M.L. *Human Resource Management in the Multinational Company.* New York: Nichols, 1977.

5. Franko, Lawrence G. "Who Manages Multinational Enterprises?" *Columbia Journal of World Business* 8, no. 2, (Summer 1973).

6. Harris, Philip R., and Moran, Robert T. *Managing Cultural Differences.* Houston: Gulf, 1979.

7. Heller, Jean E. "Criteria for Selecting an International Manager." *Personnel* 57 (May–June 1980).

8. Howard, Cecil G. "The Multinational Corporation: Impact on Nativization." *Personnel*, January–February 1972.

9. Illman, Paul E. *Developing Overseas Managers—And Managers Overseas.* New York: AMACOM, 1980.

10. Lanier, Alison, R. "Selecting and Preparing Personnel for Overseas Transfers." *Personnel Journal*, March 1979.

11. LaPalombara, Joseph, and Blank, Stephen. *Multinational Corporations and National Elites: A Study of Tensions.* New York: The Conference Board, 1976.

12. Maddox, Robert C. "Solving the Overseas Personnel Problem." *Personnel Journal*, June 1975.

13. McClenahen, John S. "The Overseas Manager: Not Actually A World Away." *Industry Week*, November 1, 1976.

14. Miller, Edwin L., and Cheng, Joseph L.C. "A Closer Look at the Decision to Accept an Overseas Position." *Management International Review* 18 (1978).

15. Perlmutter, Howard W. "The Fortuitous Evolution of the Multinational Corporation." *Columbia Journal of World Business*, January–February 1969.

16. Phatak, Arvind V. *Managing Multinational Corporations.* New York: Praeger Publishers, 1974.

17. Rose, Stanford. "The Rewarding Strategies of Multinationalism." *Fortune*, 15 September 1968.

18. Smith, Lee. "The Hazards of Coming Home." *Dun's Review*, October 1975.

19. Tung, Rosalie L. "U.S. Multinationals: A Study of Their Selection and Training Procedures for Overseas Assignments." *Academy of Management Proceedings*, 1979.

20. Voris, William. "Considerations in Staffing for Overseas Management Needs." *Personnel Journal*, June 1975.

21. Young, David. "Fair Compensation for Expatriates." *Harvard Business Review*, July–August 1973.

22. Zeria, Yoram, and Harari, Ehud. "Genuine Multinational Staffing Policy: Expectations and Realities." *Academy of Management Journal* 20, no. 2 (1977).

NOTES

1. Edwin L. Miller and Joseph L.C. Cheng, "A Closer Look at the Decision to Accept an Overseas Position," *Management International Review* 18, (1978): 25–27.

2. Rosalie L. Tung, "U.S. Multinationals: A Study of Their Selection and Training Procedures for Overseas Assignments," *Academy of Management Proceedings*, 1979, p. 298.

3. Ibid.

4. R.L. Desatnick and M.L. Bennett, *Human Resource Management in the Multinational Company* (New York: Nichols Publishing Co. 1977), pp. 233–34.

5. Sanford Rose, "The Rewarding Strategies of Multinationalism," *Fortune*, 15 September 1968, p. 180.

6. Ibid.

7. Ibid.

8. Cecil G. Howard, "The Multinational Corporation: Impact on Nativization," *Personnel*, January–February 1972, p. 42.

9. Tung, "U.S. Multinationals."

10. Joseph LaPalombara and Stephen Blank, *Multinational Corporations and National Elites: A Study of Tensions* (New York: The Conference Board, 1976), p. 57.

11. Lawrence G. Franko, "Who Manages Multinational Enterprises?" *Columbia Journal of World Consumers* 8, no. 2 (Summer 1973): 30–42.

12. Ibid., p. 39.

13. Ibid.

14. Ibid.

5. International Staffing

15. "American Standard's Executive Melting Pot," *Business Week*, 2 July 1979, p. 93.
16. Jean E. Heller, "Criteria for Selecting an International Manager," *Personnel* 57 (May–June 1980): 48.
17. Ibid.
18. Arvind V. Phatak, *Managing Multinational Corporations* (New York: Praeger Publishers, 1974), p. 194.
19. William Voris, "Considerations in Staffing for Overseas Management Needs," *Personnel Journal*, June 1975, p. 354.
20. Heller, "Criteria for Selecting an International Manager," p. 49.
21. Robert C. Maddox, "Solving the Overseas Personnel Problem," *Personnel Journal* 44, no. 2 (February 1965): 93.
22. "Gauging a Family's Suitability for a Stint Overseas," *Business Week*, 16 April 1979, p. 127.
23. Tung, "U.S. Multinationals," pp. 298–299.
24. "Gauging a Family's Suitability," pp. 127–30.
25. Alison R. Lanier, "Selecting and Preparing Personnel for Overseas Transfers," *Personnel Journal* 58 (March 1979): 162–63.
26. Philip R. Harris and Robert T. Moran, *Managing Cultural Differences* (Houston: Gulf Publishing Co. 1979), p. 149.
27. Ibid., pp. 128–29. Reprinted by permission.
28. "How to Ease Re-entry After Overseas Duty," *Business Week*, 11 June 1979, p. 82.
29. John S. McClenahan, "The Overseas Manager: Not Actually a World Away," *Industry Week*, 1 November 1976, p. 53.
30. Ibid.
31. Lee Smith, "The Hazards of Coming Home," *Dun's Review*, October 1975, p. 72.
32. "How to Ease Re-entry."
33. Ibid., p. 84.
34. McClenahan, "The Overseas Manager," p. 53.
35. Desatnick and Bennett, *Human Resource Management*, p. 168.
36. Paul E. Illman, *Developing Overseas Managers—And Managers Overseas* (New York: AMACOM, 1980), p. 178.
37. Ibid., p. 176.
38. Howard W. Perlmutter, "The Tortuous Evolution of the Multinational Corporation," *Columbia Journal of World Business* 3, no. 1 (January–February 1969): 11–14.
39. W.A. Borrman, "The Problem of Expatriate Personnel and Their Selection in International Enterprises," *Management International Review* 8, no. 4–5 (1968): 37–38.
40. Yoram Zeira and Ehud Harari, "Genuine Multinational Staffing Policy: Expectations and Realities," *Academy of Management Journal* 20, no. 2 (1977): 328.
41. Borrman, "The Problem of Expatriate Personnel," p. 40.
42. Graef S. Crystal, *Compensating U.S. Expatriates Abroad: An AMA Management Briefing* (New York: American Management Association, 1972), pp. 1–3.

43. E.J. Kolde, *The Multinational Company* (Lexington, Mass.: Lexington Books, 1974), pp. 176–78.
44. Ibid., pp. 178–79.
45. Ibid., pp. 179–80.
46. Ibid., pp. 180–81.
47. *Compensating International Executives* (New York: Business International Corporation, 1970), p. 33.
48. Ibid.
49. Ibid.
50. Crystal, *Compensating U.S. Expatriates Abroad*, p. 44.
51. Ibid.
52. Ibid., p. 9.
53. David Young, "Fair Compensation for Expatriates," *Harvard Business Review* 51, no. 4 (July–August 1973): 119.
54. Ibid., pp. 119–20.
55. Ibid., pp. 120–21.
56. *Compensating International Executives*, pp. 23–25.
57. Crystal, *Compensating U.S. Expatriates Abroad*, pp. 18–19.
58. Young, "Fair Compensation for Expatriates," pp. 123–45.
59. Ibid.
60. Ibid.
61. Crystal, *Compensating U.S. Expatriates Abroad*, p. 10.

Chapter **6**

The Control Process in an International Context

A multinational company derives its strength from being able to recognize and capitalize on opportunities anywhere in the world, and from its capacity to respond to global threats to its business operations in a timely fashion. On the basis of an evaluation of global opportunities and threats, and of the company's strengths and weaknesses, top management executives of a multinational company at the parent company level formulate the corporate strategy of the total company. The objectives of the multinational company serve as the umbrella under which the objectives of divisions and subsidiaries are developed. There is a considerable amount of give and take between the parent company, divisions, and subsidiaries before the divisional and subsidiary level objectives are finally agreed to by executives at all three levels.

The objective of managerial control is to ensure that plans are being implemented correctly. In this chapter the focus will be on the parent company's managerial control over its foreign subsidiaries. We shall examine first the salient features of the managerial control process. Then, because multinational companies experience problems controlling their far-flung operations, we shall look at the problems and their causes. The chapter next includes a review of the typical characteristics of control systems used by international companies; and it concludes with some suggestions for improving the international control process.

THE MANAGERIAL CONTROL PROCESS

Managerial control is a process directed toward ensuring that performance of operations and personnel adheres to plans. A control system is essential because the future is uncertain. Assumptions about the internal and external environment which were the basis of the forecast may prove invalid; strategies may not be applicable; budgets and programs may not be effective. Managerial control is a process that evaluates performance and takes corrective action when performance differs significantly from plans. With managerial control, any deviations from forecasts, objectives, or plans can be located early and corrected with minimum difficulty.

Managerial control involves several management skills: planning, coordinating, communicating, processing and evaluating information, and influencing people.

There are four main elements in the managerial control process.[1]

1. The setting of standards.
2. The development of monitoring devices or techniques to monitor the performance of the individual or the organizational system.
3. The comparison of performance measures obtained from the different monitoring devices to the plans in order to determine if the current state of performance is sufficiently close to the planned state.
4. The employment of effectuating or action devices that can be used to correct significant deviations of performance.

There is a close relationship between managerial control and planning. Managerial control depends on the objectives set forth in the tactical plans, which in turn are derived from the strategic plans of the organization. The tactical plans are for the short-term contributions of each functional area toward the strategic plans, goals, and objectives.

Setting the Standards

The first step in the control process is the setting of standards. These standards are derived from the objectives defined in the planning process. Without definition of objectives, there can be no formulation of standards.

After standards are formulated, a hierarchy of importance needs to be established. It would be inefficient and unrealistic to set specific standards for every organizational activity; hence management should continuously monitor performance of activities in key areas, those it considers to be essential. (Whatever is not considered essential to the attainment of the company's objectives could be controlled by "exception," in which monitoring is periodic and on a sample basis.)[2] In the key areas, the standards need to be as concrete and as specific as possible—while taking into consideration the fact that some key areas, such as management development, cannot be expressed in specific and concrete terms.[3]

Monitoring the Performance

Once the standards have been established the next step is the development of techniques to monitor and accurately describe performance.

Budgets, managerial audits, and financial statements are the main measuring devices used to measure the performance of organizational systems. A budget is a "detailed listing of the resources or money assigned to a particular project or unit."[4] The standards for performance are translated into dollar amounts for each item in the budget. However, the dynamic, changing character of the business environment necessitates some flexibility in budgets.

There are several methods for making budgets flexible without losing managerial control over time, such as the adoption of supplemental budgets, alternative budgets, and variable expense budgets. Supplemental budgets are used with budgets that establish limits on expenditures—such as for plant expansion, capital improvements, etc. If a capital expenditure budget proves to be too low because of inaccurate costing in the planning stage, a supplemental budget would be prepared and added to the original budget.[5]

Alternative budgeting is another form of controlled budgeting. A budget is prepared on the basis of the organization's assessment of the most probable future conditions. However, if there is a real possibility that, for example, sales may be lower (or higher), alternative budgets are also prepared, based on the implications of the specific lower or higher sales figures.

A third type of budgeting is the variable expense budget, a type found mostly in manufacturing organizations. Variable expense budgets are devised to ensure proper coordination of activities as changes take place in sales of manufactured goods. These budgets are "schedules of costs of production that tell managers what levels of critical activities actually should be established as changes occur in sales and output volume."[6]

All these budgetary techniques require accurate and timely communication. Variable expense budgets, in particular, depend on accurate and prompt reports from production and sales.

Another typical control mechanism of the organizational systems are financial statements—particularly the income statement, which details the sources of revenues and expenses for a given year, the profit and loss statement, balance sheets, and so on.

Comparing Performance to Plans

The third step in the managerial control process is comparing the performance measures obtained from the different monitoring devices to the objectives, and evaluating whether the current state is sufficiently close to the planned state. Management must decide how much variation between the standard and actual performance is tolerable, and what is "sufficiently close" for the organization.

Changes in the external environment may affect the limits of possible performance, which in turn may necessitate a change in the performance standards. Once the limits of the possible are altered, management must decide how the standards of measurement should be altered. Naturally, when the external environment does not deviate from the forecast, the task of managerial control is simply to evaluate whether performance is within acceptable limits.

Another aspect of the evaluation step in the control process has to do with feedback and feedforward controls. In *feedback* controls, the focus is on information about events that have already occurred (such as production, actual sales). This information is compared with the standard in order to make necessary corrections in the future. For example, feedback control is typically used to monitor the productivity and performance of a factory worker against a preset production rate.

Feedforward controls are different in that the deviations from standards are anticipated or predicted before they occur. When the anticipated conditions do occur, certain actions are scheduled to take place in anticipation of the outcome of the first occurrence. For example, when sales volume reaches a predetermined level, management will be obliged to automatically increase the level of inventory (this action is taken to prevent inventories from running out, which would otherwise logically occur as the result of the first occurrence, the sales increase). "Feedback control cures problems; feedforward control prevents them."[7] Companies use both types of controls, although feedback is more common because it is less complicated and requires less forecasting.

From the discussion so far, it is apparent that accurate communication and a pervasive managerial information system is essential in management control. Management cannot appraise, compare, or correct performance without proper reporting of appropriate and meaningful information.

Correcting the Deviations

The fourth step in the control process is correcting significant deviations from standard, for which effectuating or action devices must be employed. The application of action devices requires many management skills—such as decision making, persuading, effectively communicating, etc. When a subsystem of an organization needs help, the corrective action might be to use different budgeting techniques, or to impose control mechanisms on costs, expenses, and so on. When the deviation concerns organizational personnel, the action devices could be either positive (promotions, salary increases, increased responsibility and special privileges) or negative (reprimands, withdrawal of privileges, demotions, salary reductions, and termination from employment).[8]

It is essential to recognize the overriding human dimension in the managerial control process. The steps or elements in the control process are not automatic, but are activated by management. Monitoring, comparing, and action devices depend on human intervention. The necessary communication is between people. The effectiveness of the control system depends on the acceptance of the system as necessary, legitimate, and appropriate by the members of the organization. This human dimension is most significant in the managerial process in a multinational company.

THE PROBLEMS OF CONTROL IN AN INTERNATIONAL COMPANY

Control and the problems associated with it are far more complex in a multinational company than in one that is purely domestic because the multinational operates in more than one cultural, economic, political, and legal environment. Let us examine a few of the most important international variables having a major negative impact on the flow of information between the headquarters and subsidiaries; this block, we shall see, in turn influences the effectiveness of the multinational company's control system.

Despite the sophistication and speed of contemporary communication systems, *geographic distance* between the parent and the foreign affiliate continues to cause communication distortion. Differences in language between the parent company and its foreign affiliates are also responsible for the distortions in communication. *Language barriers* caused by language differences involve both the content and the meaning of the messages. Many ideas and concepts are not easily translatable from one language to another. Because of geographic distances, there is little face to face communication and the messages of nonverbal communication are lost.

Problems are also caused by misunderstanding the *communications habits* of people in other cultures. Managers of different cultures may interact and yet may block out important messages because the manner in which the message is presented may mean something different to the sending and receiving cultures. For example, a manager may make a wrong judgment about a subordinate's performance because he or she is unaware of culturally different communications habits. As an illustration, consider that the aborigines in Australia exhibit attention by listening intently with their faces and bodies turned away from the speaker, and with no eye contact.[9] This behavior could easily be misread by a member of a different culture, one who is accustomed to associate body posture and eye contact with attention.

Cultural distance is as significant as geographic distance in creating communication distortions. Lack of understanding and acceptance of the cultural values of a group may impair a manager's ability to evaluate information accurately, to judge performance fairly, and to make valid decisions about this performance. This failure could create problems in a multinational company in the area of employee performance appraisal.

In some cultures one does not make criticism bluntly, but discusses critical areas in an oblique fashion. And in the Mexican culture, responsibility is viewed as being tied to fate. It is therefore deeply offensive to a Mexican to be told that he or she is personally responsible for some failure.[10] In contrast, the American style of managerial control fixes responsibilities for achieving certain organizational goals on specific members in the organization. Other control mechanisms are also affected by cultural differences. The detailed reporting required by some "tight" managerial control systems is not acceptable to some cultures. Also, the degree of harmony valued in a culture may make the accurate reporting of problems difficult.[11]

For example, in the Japanese culture, maintaining group cohesiveness is considered to be far more important than reporting a problem to a superior who would place the blame on the group or an individual within the group. It is therefore not unusual for Japanese supervisors *not* to report a problem to upper management in the hope that it can be solved at the group level.

Communication distortion between the parent company and a foreign affiliate may occur because of the *differing frames of reference* of these two organizational units. The parent company may perceive each foreign affiliate as just one of many and therefore may have a tendency to view each affiliate's problems in light of the company's entire global network of operations. However, the foreign affiliate head may view the problems of his operations as very important to him and to his affiliate. Both the parent company and affiliate head may try to communicate their feelings and views to each other without much success because each could be communicating from a different frame of reference.

THE CHARACTERISTICS OF CONTROL SYSTEMS IN INTERNATIONAL COMPANIES

Multinational companies use a variety of control systems to monitor and change the performance of their foreign subsidiaries. Some of these controls are *direct* controls whereas others can be categorized as *indirect*.

Direct Controls

Direct controls include the use of such devices as periodic meetings, visits by home country executives to foreign affiliates, and staffing of foreign affiliates by home country nationals. Control can be exercised by holding management meetings to discuss the performance of foreign affiliates.

Some companies, such as International Telephone and Telegraph Corporation, hold monthly management meetings at the headquarters in New York at which each ITT manager of every profit-and-loss division, however small, is in attendance. The meeting is presided over by the chief executive officer of the company, and reports submitted by each ITT unit head from around the world are discussed. Each report contains all facts concerning the performance of the unit—such as financial analyses of sales, profits, return on investment, and virtually every other measurement used in business. The report is also expected to contain a description of every existing and potential problem affecting the operation. Description of the problem, however, is not enough. It must also explain how and why the problem arose and how the executive in charge of the unit plans on solving it. Other multinational companies also resort to meetings, similar to ITT's, for controlling their foreign affiliates. The focus of such meetings is on direct face-to-face communications and direct feedback.

Visits by top executives from the corporate headquarters to each foreign affiliate also serve as control devices. It is not unusual for the chief executive officer and a group of top headquarters executives to spend several days sitting across the table each month from subsidiary and regional managers. Such visits are held so that problems can be dealt with up close—competition problems, performance problems, or others.

The international staffing practices of some multinational companies are also aimed at ensuring adequate control over the foreign affiliates. The practice adopted by many companies of staffing the top management slot of a foreign subsidiary by a manager from the home country is for this purpose. Whether the reason is a lack of trust of foreign nationals or a belief that home country nationals are better managers and more knowledgeable about the company's overall philosophies, policies, and strategies than are managers of foreign nationality, putting a home country national in charge of a foreign subsidiary is supposed to provide the subsidiary with the type and kind of management that the parent company wants. The idea is that the better that a foreign subsidiary is managed, the fewer its deviations of performance from planned performance, and therefore the fewer the problems associated with controlling its operations.

The organization structure of the company is yet another control mechanism. In an earlier chapter we examined the various types of organizational structures that multinational companies have used to coordinate and control their global operations. No two companies have the same organizational structure because the companies need different types of information flows in order to control their far-flung operations. For example, the creation of regional management units in a product division structure reflects an attempt by companies to shorten the distance between the headquarters and foreign affiliates, thereby promoting better control over foreign operations.

Indirect Controls

The preceding paragraphs dealt with the so-called direct controls. Companies also use indirect controls to control foreign subsidiaries. These include the various reports each foreign subsidiary is expected to submit to top management detailing its performance during a certain period, similar to those required by ITT from each foreign unit head. Other forms of indirect controls include a whole range of budgetary and financial controls, which are imposed through budgets and various types of financial statements such as the balance sheet, profit-and-loss statement, cash budget, and an exhaustive set of financial ratios depicting the financial health of the subsidiary.

Most companies use returns on investment and profits as the dominant criteria for the evaluation of the performance of a foreign affiliate. A study conducted by Robbins and Stobaugh of 150 companies with foreign operations showed that 95 percent of them judged their foreign subsidiaries on precisely the same basis as the domestic subsidiaries and almost without exception, they use a form of ROI (return on investment) as the main measure of performance.[12] However, the reported profits of a foreign subsidiary and its ROI may not, and very rarely do, reflect its true performance. What follows is a discussion of why this is the case.

MEASURES OF PERFORMANCE: REPORTED PROFITS AND ROI

There are many decisions made above the subsidiary level—at the parent company or regional headquarters—which affect the operations of the subsidiary. Take, for example, the manipulation by the parent company or regional headquarters of transfer prices of raw materials, components, or products in intracompany transactions. A higher-than-arm's-length price might be charged on exports made by a subsidiary located in a low–income tax country to a subsidiary located in a country that has high income tax rates. Other things being equal, this would result in lower profits in the importing subsidiary, and therefore lower taxes; and higher profits in the exporting subsidiary. However, the important point is that the difference in tax rates could result in maximizing corporate profits.

Transfer prices are manipulated upward or downward depending on whether the parent company wishes to inject or remove cash into or from a subsidiary. Prices on imports by a subsidiary from a related subsidiary are raised if the multinational company wishes to move funds from the receiver to the seller, but they are lowered if the objective is to keep the funds in the importing subsidiary. Similarly, prices on exports from a subsidiary to a related subsidiary are raised if the multinational company wishes to move funds from the importer to the exporter. Multinational companies have been known to use transfer pricing for moving excess cash from subsidiaries located in countries with weak currencies to countries with strong currencies in order to protect the value of their current assets.

Transfer prices are also manipulated in order to give a better credit rating to a foreign subsidiary. Showing that a subsidiary has a good record of earnings makes it easier for it to borrow money in the local money markets.

These are some of the ways in which transfer prices are used advantageously by multinational companies. However, transfer prices can create serious internal management control problems, because the manipulation of transfer prices forces the subsidiaries it affects to show profits that are allocated to them rather than actually earned by them. Hence, allocated profits reported by subsidiaries should not be used to measure their performance, because they do not reflect the real performance of the subsidiaries being monitored.

It is possible that a foreign country could have severe inflation for months or years without any devaluation of its currency. This could help a subsidiary in that country to earn high profits, but they would rightly be attributable to the high inflation rate rather than good management. On the other hand, when devaluation of the local currency vis-à-vis the U.S. dollar does occur within a given accounting period, the subsidiary, although well managed and profitable in terms of the local currency, may show a loss when its income statement is translated into U.S. dollars. This situation could result in a faulty evaluation of the subsidiary's management. What further complicates this problem is that, although inflation and devaluation generally tend to be approximately equal in magnitude in the long run, they are rarely exactly equal within a given period of time. More often than not, devaluations are inappropriate to compensate for the domestic inflation.

The profitability criterion may have to be modified for a subsidiary that is located in a country whose government lets it be known that it expects the subsidiary to make positive contributions to the nation's economy. This requirement may compel the subsidiary to engage in activities that may not contribute to its short-run profitability, such as the maximum use of locally produced components (even though they may not meet the quality requirements) and a no-layoff policy for the labor force.

There are many companywide logistics decisions that are actually made above the subsidiary level but which do affect the subsidiary's profitability for better or worse. For example, executives at the parent company level might decide to serve third markets that were previously served by subsidiary A by exports from subsidiary B. This would adversely affect the sales volume and consequently the profits of subsidiary A. It would therefore be erroneous to assume that the reported profits of subsidiary A and subsidiary B reflect the performance of their respective managements—without taking into consideration the impact on the subsidiaries' operations of the parent company's decision to shift exports to third markets from subsidiary A to subsidiary B.

DESIGNING AN EFFECTIVE INTERNATIONAL CONTROL SYSTEM

An effective control system cannot rely upon reported profits and ROI as the dominant measures of performance of a foreign subsidiary because the corporate headquarters of the company rather than the subsidiary manager makes most of the major decisions affecting the profitability of the subsidiary. To obtain a more accurate picture of a subsidiary's performance one must be certain to eliminate extraneous factors—results, positive or negative, caused by decisions made above the subsidiary level, or results due to environmental variables, such as unprecedented fluctuations in the price of raw materials (for example, the unexpected sharp increase in the price of petroleum in 1974) or due to government actions, over which the subsidiary management could not exercise any control. Thus, a subsidiary manager should be held accountable for results that were caused by actions that he could initiate, without external interference, and by decisions that he could make unilaterally.

The profit-and-loss statement or the ROI of the subsidiary should be adjusted to reflect its actual performance, taking into account the above-mentioned factors. It is quite conceivable, under such a system, for a subsidiary manager to be rated quite favorably in spite of his having reported a poor profit-and-loss statement. And the opposite is also possible. A manager who shows huge profits may still be judged to be a poor manager if his performance warrants such a judgment.

In addition to the financial measures, the assessment should also use nonfinancial measures of performance—such as market share, productivity, relations with the host country government, public image, employee morale, union relations, community involvement, and so on. Most companies do take into account some nonfinancial factors; however it might be advisable to formalize the process, with scorecard ratings for all subsidiaries based on the same broad range of variables.

Finally, the level of performance expected from a foreign subsidiary in the following year should consider the characteristics of its environment and how it is likely to change from this year. Thus, an environment that was generally favorable this year might be expected to change for the worse the following year; hence, the level of performance expected should be appropriately lowered as well. Not doing so could lead to unhealthy pressure on the subsidiary manager, perhaps inducing him to make decisions about maintenance expenditures or service to customers or funding of process improvements that are detrimental in the long run to both the subsidiary and the multinational company as a whole.

SUMMARY

In this chapter we looked at the managerial control process in an international context. The focus was on the problems and characteristics of control systems adopted by multinational companies in order to manage their foreign subsidiaries, with emphasis on ways to improve the process.

Managerial control is the process of ensuring that actual performance is equal to the planned performance. The purpose of control is to facilitate the implementation of plans by continuously monitoring the performance of the people responsible for carrying them out.

There are four principal elements in the control process: (1) establishing standards against which performance is to be measured; (2) developing devices or techniques to monitor individual or organizational performance; (3) comparing actual performance with the planned performance; (4) taking corrective action to eliminate significant deviations of performance from plans.

The process of control and the problems associated with it are far more complex in a multinational company than in its purely domestic counterpart because of the multiple cultural, economic, political, and legal environments that its subsidiaries operate in. Several divisive factors—such as geographic distance, language barriers, cultural distance, and differing frames of reference—between the parent company and foreign subsidiary managers are responsible for distortion in the information which is required for control purposes.

Multinational companies use several forms of monitoring devices to control their foreign subsidiaries. Among the so-called direct controls commonly used are periodic meetings at the headquarters between subsidiary and regional heads and corporate executives; visits by corporate executives to foreign affiliates; staffing subsidiaries by home country nationals, and the organizational structure. Indirect controls include such devices as periodic reports from subsidiaries, detailing their performance for the given period; a whole range of financial controls, such as budgetary control and financial statements; and financial ratios that depict the financial health of an operating unit.

Most companies use profits and return-on-investment figures as the two dominant criteria to evaluate the performance of subsidiaries. However, these measures may not accurately reflect the real performance level of a subsidiary because corporate or regional managers—not the subsidiary manager—make many significant decisions that affect the subsidiary's performance. Besides there are several forces in the subsidiary's environment which the subsidiary manager cannot control and which significantly affect, favorably or unfavorably, the subsidiary's performance. Therefore, the profit-and-loss statement or the ROI of a foreign subsidiary should be adjusted to reflect its actual performance by removing from consideration positive or negative results that were due to forces or factors beyond the control of the subsidiary manager.

Nonfinancial measures—such as market share and productivity—should be used in conjunction with the financial measures. And the performance level expected from a subsidiary should change from year to year depending on the characteristics of the environment that it will have to operate in from one year to the next.

QUESTIONS

1. Why is the control process more difficult to implement in a multinational company as opposed to a purely domestic company? Discuss factors that influence the effectiveness of a multinational company's control system.

2. What are direct and indirect controls? Give examples.

3. Explain why the reported profits of a foreign affiliate may not be a good measure of its true performance.

4. What are the essential features of a sound international control system?

FURTHER READING

1. Clutterbuck, David. "Breaking Through the Cultural Barriers." *International Management*, December 1980.

2. Drucker, Peter F. *An Introductory View of Management*. New York: Harper & Row, 1977.

3. Gannon, Martin J. *Management: An Organizational Perspective.* Boston: Little, Brown, 1977.

4. Phatak, Arvind V. *Managing Multinational Corporations,* New York: Praeger Publishers, 1974.

5. Robbins, Sydney M. and Stobaugh, Robert B. "The Broad Measuring Stick for Foreign Subsidiaries." *Harvard Business Review,* September–October 1973.

6. Steiner, George. *Strategic Planning.* New York: The Free Press, 1979.

NOTES

1. Martin J. Gannon, *Management: An Organizational Perspective* (Boston: Little, Brown, 1977), p. 140.
2. Peter F. Drucker, *An Introductory View of Management* (New York: Harper & Row, 1977), p. 424.
3. George A. Steiner, *Strategic Planning* (New York: The Free Press, 1979), p. 268.
4. Gannon, *Management: An Organizational Perspective,* p. 143.
5. Steiner, *Strategic Planning,* p. 220.
6. Ibid., p. 221.
7. Gannon, *Management: An Organizational Perspective,* p. 141.
8. Ibid., p. 157.
9. David Clutterbuck, "Breaking Through the Cultural Barriers," *International Management,* December 1980, p. 41.
10. Ibid.
11. Arvind V. Phatak, *Managing Multinational Corporations* (New York: Praeger Publishers, 1974), p. 225.
12. Sydney M. Robbins and Robert B. Stobaugh, "The Bent Measuring Stick for Foreign Subsidiaries," *Harvard Business Review* 51, no. 5 (September–October 1973): 82.

Index

INDEX

Culture (*cont.*)
  importance of understanding, 19–20
  meaning of, 20–21
Currency instability, as environmental issue, 42, 138
Customers, following of, as reason for foreign production, 15–16

Deadlines, need for, by Americans, 25
Devaluation of currency, and inflation, as management control problems, 138
Diplomatic skills, of manager, 99
Distribution, effective channels of, necessity of, 54
Domestic companies
  monitoring of environment, 41
  organizational structure of, 65
Domestic market, size of, as reason for foreign production, 16
Domestic units, integrating of, 44

Economic development, level of, as important dimension, 57
Economics, definition of, 30
Education allowances, 120
Emotional maturity and stability, of overseas managers, 100
Empathy, cultural, 98
Employees, classification of, for compensation system, 117
Environment
  constraints of, and strengths and weaknesses of company, relation between, 54–55, 55
  external, changing of, importance of, 52
  future, as influence on subsidiary performance, 139–40
  international, 5–7, 6
  unfamiliar, adaptability of family to, 101
Environmental analysis, 49–52
Environmental assessment task, importance of, 45
Environmental factors, for market entry strategies, 54
Environmental information, internalizing of, 45
Environmental issues, in international planning
  external, 41–43
  internal, 43–46
Environmental problems, in international planning
  external, 41–43
  internal, 41, 43–46
Ethnocentric attitude, of international company, 113
European Economic Community (EEC), 15
Exchange rates, fluctuations in, 121
Executives, international
  compensation of, 115–21
  primary attitudes of, 113
Export, 7
  inhouse manager of, 69
Export department, of international company, 10–11
Export manager, in international company, 10

Failures, managerial, abroad, avoidance of, 90
Family, of manager, 100–102
Feedback controls, in managerial control process, 131
Feedforward controls, as evaluation step in control process, 132
Financial statement, as control mechanism, 131
Flexibility, as desirable trait of manager, 98–99
Foreign affiliates

direct control over, staffing for, 135–36
  in international company, 13–14
Foreign assignments
  criteria for selecting managers for, 97–102
  managerial categories of, 101–2
  preparation of manager for, 104–8
  selection methods for, 102–4
Foreign markets
  sales forecasts, importance of, 46
  timing of entry into, 47
  value of entry into, evaluation of, 48–49
Foreign nationals, as managers, 96–97
Foreign units, integration of, as environmental issue, 44
Frames of reference, differing, as problem in international company, 134

Geocentric attitude, of international company, 113–14
Geographic distance, as problem for international company, 133
Geography
  as dimension of international business, 56
  as factor in coordinating global operations, 79
Global structures
  advantages of, 81
  area division of, 79–82, 80
  companies most adaptable to, 81
  corporate decisions in, 76
  decisions for, 75–76
  disadvantages of, 81–82
  domestic market for, as one of many, 79–80
  functional division of, 82–84, 83
  global responsibility in, 75–76
  matrix structure within (*see* Matrix structure)
  multidimensional, 84–87, 86
  new organizational structure of, 76
  product division of, 76–79, 77
  products at maturity stage in, 80–81
  use of company resources by, 76

Home countries, foreign managers at headquarters in, 96–97
Home country nationals, as managers
  assignment of, 95
  definition of, 91, 122
  in European companies, 95
  importance of quality, 97
  objective for hiring, 91, 92
  product line strategy of, 95
  replacement of, 95
Home leaves, 120
Host country nationals
  compensation of, 121
  definition of, 91, 122
  as managers
    advantages of, 111
    facts determining selection of, 93–94
    positions held by, 93, 96
    reasons for hiring of, 94–95
    recruitment and selection of, 111–13
    replacing home country nationals, 96
    use of, in advanced regions, 94
    recruitment and selection of, 111–12
Host country welfare plans, reimbursement for payments into, 118–19
Housing allowance, 119

INDEX

INDEX

Management
  definition of, 2–3
  international (*see* International management)
  meetings, as direct control, 135
  need for, 3
Managerial control
  management skills required for, 129
  objective of, 128
  and planning, 129
  process, 129–33, 140
  purpose of, 140
Managerial skills, as desirable trait of manager, 98
Managers
  ability of, to think and act on companywide basis, 45
  adaptable, search for, 77
  Americans abroad, top level, policies of, 93
  area, in global structure, 80
  ensuring foreign operations contributions, importance of, 59
  export, of international company, 10
  for foreign assignments, criteria for, 97–102
  foreign nationals as, at home country headquarters, 96–97
  home country nationals as (*see* Home country nationals, as managers)
  host country nationals as (*see* Host country nationals, as managers)
  inhouse export, 69
  international
    adaptability of family of, 100–102
    adaptability and flexibility of, 98–99
    anxiety of returning home, reasons for, 108–9
    autonomy of, 109
    cultural empathy of, 98
    desirable traits in, 97–102, 122
    diplomatic skills of, 99
    emotional stability and maturity of, 100
    environment of, 5
    failure of, consequences of, 109
    financial burdens of, upon returning home, 109
    functions of, 3, 7
    language aptitude of, 99–101
    managerial skills of, 98
    monitoring and surveillance by, 7
    need to analyze cultural differences, 29
    personal motives of, 100
    preparing for foreign assignment, 104–8
    problems posed by language and, 27–29
    repatriating of, 108–11
    responsibilities of, 5–7
    study of environmental variables by, 7
    technical ability of, 98
    training programs for, 104–8
  with international perspective, developing of, 45
  isolation of, in international division structure, 73
  knowledge and appreciation needed by, 45
  in matrix structure, 86–87
  product division, motivation of, 79
  selection of, for international staffing, 135–36
  sources of, 91
  subsidiary, 44, 85
  third country nationals as, 92–93
Man and the universe, as dimension of culture, 30
Manufacturing
  contract, 8, 12
  foreign, 9
  investment in, by international company, 12–13

Marketing
  inhouse export manager as adjunct to, 69
  in Islamic culture, 32–35
Markets
  domestic, 16, 79–80, *80*
  entry, *53*, 57
  foreign, 15, 70
Material culture, as dimension of culture, 29–30
Materialism, of Americans, 23–24
Matrix structure, 85–87, *86*
Meetings
  business, effect of cultural differences in, 23
  management, as direct control, 135
Monitoring, in managerial control process, 130–31
Multinational companies. *See* International companies

National governments, pressures from, as environmental issue, 42
Nationalism, as environmental issue, 43

Objectives, of international company, 58–59, *58*
Organizational structures, 66, 87, 136. *See also* specific structures ˙
Organizations, purpose of, 65
Overseas managerial assignments, categories of, 101–2
Overseas premium (OP), 118
Ownership, as dimension of international business, 57

Patent protection, as environmental issue, 43
Performance
  compared to plans, in managerial control process, 131–32
  measures of, 136–38
  monitoring of, in mangerial control process, 130–31
  past, as selection method for foreign assignment, 102–3
Perquisites, 120
Personal motives, as desirable trait, 100
Philosophies, staffing, multinational, 113–15
Planning
  definitions of, 40
  ineffective, poor allocation of resources in, 47
  lack of, consequences of, 46–48
  managerial control and, 129
Plans, compared to performance, in mangerial control process, 131–32
Political instability, as environmental issue, 41–42
Polycentric attitude, of international company, 113
Portfolio investment, 8
Pre-departure program, 122
Prices
  export, income tax rates and, 137
  transfer, 137–38
Pricing, transfer, as cause for divisionalization, 73–74
Problems
  operational, in lack of planning, 47–48
  reporting of, as difficult in some cultures, 134
Product committees, 84
Product cycle, 67, *68*
Product division, global. *See* Global structures, product division of
Production